Daniel Butnaru

Computational Steering with Reduced Complexity

Daniel Butnaru

Computational Steering with Reduced Complexity

Südwestdeutscher Verlag für Hochschulschriften

Impressum / Imprint

Bibliografische Information der Deutschen Nationalbibliothek: Die Deutsche Nationalbibliothek verzeichnet diese Publikation in der Deutschen Nationalbibliografie; detaillierte bibliografische Daten sind im Internet über http://dnb.d-nb.de abrufbar.

Alle in diesem Buch genannten Marken und Produktnamen unterliegen warenzeichen-, marken- oder patentrechtlichem Schutz bzw. sind Warenzeichen oder eingetragene Warenzeichen der jeweiligen Inhaber. Die Wiedergabe von Marken, Produktnamen, Gebrauchsnamen, Handelsnamen, Warenbezeichnungen u.s.w. in diesem Werk berechtigt auch ohne besondere Kennzeichnung nicht zu der Annahme, dass solche Namen im Sinne der Warenzeichen- und Markenschutzgesetzgebung als frei zu betrachten wären und daher von jedermann benutzt werden dürften.

Bibliographic information published by the Deutsche Nationalbibliothek: The Deutsche Nationalbibliothek lists this publication in the Deutsche Nationalbibliografie; detailed bibliographic data are available in the Internet at http://dnb.d-nb.de.

Any brand names and product names mentioned in this book are subject to trademark, brand or patent protection and are trademarks or registered trademarks of their respective holders. The use of brand names, product names, common names, trade names, product descriptions etc. even without a particular marking in this works is in no way to be construed to mean that such names may be regarded as unrestricted in respect of trademark and brand protection legislation and could thus be used by anyone.

Coverbild / Cover image: www.ingimage.com

Verlag / Publisher:
Südwestdeutscher Verlag für Hochschulschriften
ist ein Imprint der / is a trademark of
OmniScriptum GmbH & Co. KG
Heinrich-Böcking-Str. 6-8, 66121 Saarbrücken, Deutschland / Germany
Email: info@svh-verlag.de

Herstellung: siehe letzte Seite /
Printed at: see last page
ISBN: 978-3-8381-3743-8

Zugl. / Approved by: München, TU, Diss., 2013

Copyright © 2013 OmniScriptum GmbH & Co. KG
Alle Rechte vorbehalten. / All rights reserved. Saarbrücken 2013

CONTENTS

1 INTRODUCTION   1

2 TECHNIQUES FOR REDUCING THE COMPLEXITY OF SIMULATIONS   5
   2.1 Surrogates for Computational Simulations   5
   2.2 Classification of Surrogate Models   6
   2.3 Offline - Online Pattern   7
   2.4 Non-Intrusive Surrogate Models   9
      2.4.1 Kriging   9
      2.4.2 Non-Intrusive Polynomial Chaos   11
      2.4.3 Stochastic Collocation   12
   2.5 Intrusive Surrogate Models   12
      2.5.1 Reduction of a Linear System   15
      2.5.2 Reduction of a Non-Linear System   16
   2.6 Summary   17

3 REDUCING COMPLEXITY WITH SPARSE GRIDS   19
   3.1 Sparse Grids in a Nutshell   19
   3.2 Adaptive Sparse Grids   24

4 INSIGHT THROUGH INTERACTIVE COMPUTATIONAL STEERING   27
   4.1 Classical Steering Approaches   27
   4.2 Extending Steering Approaches with an Approximation Layer   29
   4.3 Steering and Insight   30

5 INTERACTIVE COMPUTATIONAL STEERING WITH SURROGATE MODELS   31
   5.1 Requirements and Challenges   31
   5.2 Non-Intrusive: Sparse Grids as Surrogate Models   33
      5.2.1 Offline Phase   33
      5.2.2 Online Phase   35
      5.2.3 Visual Analytics for Steering   37
   5.3 Model Improvement through Adaptive Refinement   38
      5.3.1 Refinement Procedure   39
      5.3.2 Refinement Criteria   40
   5.4 Steering with Intrusive Surrogate Models   43
      5.4.1 Offline Phase   44
      5.4.2 Online Phase   44
      5.4.3 Improvement Through DEIM Locality   45
   5.5 Summary   49

6	SYSTEM DESIGN		51
	6.1 System Architecture for Efficient Data Delivery		51
		6.1.1 GPU Repository	53
		6.1.2 CPU-Only Repository	55
		6.1.3 Distributed Snapshots for Large Repositories	56
		6.1.4 Visualization Requirements and Interface	56
	6.2 Performance		58
		6.2.1 GPU-Based Evaluation and Hierarchization	59
		6.2.2 Data Assembly	60
		6.2.3 Performance Summary	61
	6.3 Summary		62
7	APPLICATION STEERING		63
	7.1 Technical Aspects		63
	7.2 Evaluation Criteria		65
	7.3 Thermal Block		65
	7.4 Acoustic Horn		70
	7.5 Flow Through Building Infrastructure		72
		7.5.1 Surrogate Model	77
		7.5.2 Evaluation Performance	82
	7.6 Reactive Flow		83
		7.6.1 Non-Intrusive Surrogate	86
		7.6.2 Intrusive Surrogate	90
	7.7 Summary		91
8	CONCLUSIONS		95
A	VISUAL ENVIRONMENT		97
B	DEIM ENRICHMENT		101
	BIBLIOGRAPHY		103

ACRONYMS

BIM   Building Infrastructure Model
CFD   Computational Fluid Dynamics
DEIM   Discrete Empirical Interpolation Method
DoE   Design of Experiments
DoF   Degree of Freedom
IFC   Industry Foundation Classes
FRAVE   Fully Reconfigurable CAVE Environment
MPI   Message Passing Interface
NUMA   Non-Uniform Memory Access
PDE   partial differential equation
pMOR   parametrized Model Order Reduction
POD   Proper Orthogonal Decomposition
SAXPY   Single-precision real Alpha X Plus Y
SIMT   Single Instruction Multiple Thread
UML   Unified Modeling Language

INTRODUCTION

Real-time computing applications together with real-time visualization have been recently seen as a new direction in scientific computing by offering scientists and engineers assistance during design, construction, manufacturing or production phases, and even guiding medical doctors during surgery or diagnosis. With instant access to results, simulations depending on many parameters can be faster understood by deriving sensitivity measures or by visual inspection. The parameter (design) space might be large but the interactive access to solutions makes even an exhaustive investigation thinkable.

The main focus of this work is *what-if* or *sensitivity* analysis as a method to increase the understanding of relationships between input and output variables in a system or model. Such an analysis is typically performed by changing assumptions in the form of parameters and inspecting the simulation outcome. After several iterations of this process, important parameters or parameter ranges are identified and the gathered knowledge is used to support a future and faster decision process.

A what-if analysis workflow requires many simulation runs under the consideration that the computing time needed for a single simulation snapshot can be far from instant. As a consequence, for computationally expensive applications, the effectiveness of freely exploring the design space in order to identify parameter behavior is significantly limited. This work proposes solutions to this challenge, but before, some related concepts are presented that frame the current efforts.

Historically, classical computational steering has been defined as the interactive control of a running simulation. With focus on how to efficiently steer (change parameters) and move results from the computing to the visualization system, it can be seen as a natural framework also for what-if analysis. Latest developments in interactive computing – viewed as an extension to computational steering – demand close to real-time results and employ scenarios and codes which are feasible in this respect. Consequently, we are left with a broad category of simulation codes which cannot deliver fast results or would require significant optimization efforts.

Advances in the field of computational steering have also been joined by the exploration of new visualization possibilities. Moving away from single monitor visualizations, CAVE environments [19] offer immersive visualizations of high-resolution simulations. Tiled visualization systems [80] aggregate several display units into large visual surfaces which can either display a single high-resolution dataset or different linked views of the same data.

Many ideas in this work profited from the fruitful collaboration in two projects with focus on computational steering. The MAC B8 *Computational Steering* project fostered different approaches to computational steering with focus on the full processing pipeline ranging from scalable data processing workflows to interactive visualization and human-computer interaction in virtual and augmented reality environments. The KAUST-TUM partnership project K2 *Virtual Arabia* integrated high-resolution parametrized Computational Fluid Dynamics (CFD) simulations with interactive visualization requirements. What both projects had in common was the need to obtain insight in the behavior of computationally intensive simulations.

Classically, steering and visualization have involved the full simulation model. Luckily, the simulation – also called *high fidelity* model – needs not always be evaluated. Techniques for reducing the frequency or complexity of simulations and implicitly the cost have been actively pursued in the fields of optimization and uncertainty quantification [33]. *Low fidelity* or *surrogate* models have been developed for a number of simulations as low cost equivalents, which raises the question if such approaches are viable alternatives or extensions to classical computational steering. (Fig. 1 sketches the central idea).

In this work, we develop and evaluate surrogate models based on adaptive sparse grids to support what-if analysis of expensive simulations. We will consider the simulation as a function, where the parameters serve as input arguments while the snapshot (e.g., velocity or pressure field) is the output of the function. As an efficient multi-dimensional interpolation technique, sparse grids approximate the simulation function using a moderate number of snapshots. Algorithmically, the construction and interpolation with sparse grid surrogates are well suited for parallel implementation on modern SIMD architectures. To make use of these properties, we design and implement a distributed surrogate model which encapsulates construction, usage, and extension on parallel architectures. The model delivers interactive approximate snapshots to a distributed visualization even for very large snapshot sizes.

We build surrogate models for four engineering-relevant applications characterized by different numbers of parameters (2 to 5) and type (physical, boundary conditions or mesh transformations). All simulations codes solve partial differential equation (PDE) on computational grids. We investigate

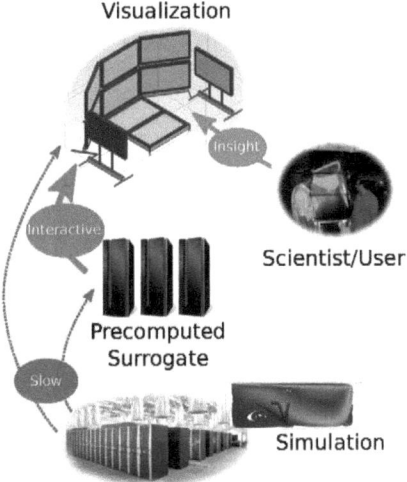

Figure 1: For a *what-if* analysis of a particular scenario many simulation codes are too slow in delivering results. The proposed solution is to pre-compute a low-fidelity representation, which can deliver approximate, but interactive results. The achieved fast response serves as input to a user-steered interactive visualization and exploration, which supports the analysis.

- a *thermal block*: heat diffusion in a plate with parametrized thermal regions,
- an *acoustic horn*: acoustic wave propagation in a narrow horn with parametrized shape,
- a *flow in a building infrastructure model (BIM)*: fluid dynamics simulation in an accurate building geometry with parametrized doors, and
- a *reactive flow*: premixed hydrogen flame with convection.

For all applications we present the accuracy of the sparse grid low-fidelity model. In terms of efficiency, a special focus is given to the evaluation for the BIM surrogate due to its large output snapshots (up to 1GB). The BIM solution is an architecture-optimized implementation stemming from a collaboration effort.

As they do not require knowledge of the PDE of the model, sparse grid surrogates are classified as *non-intrusive*. We address also *intrusive* surrogates by improving a surrogate model based on the Discrete Empirical Interpolation Method (DEIM) and apply it to the reactive flow problem.

To convey our achievements we structure this work as follows: Chap. 2 considers a formalism for surrogate models and outlines the standard *offline* (construction) and *online* (usage) phases. Guided by the distinction intrusive/non-intrusive we discuss the computational requirements for a set of popular surrogates in the context of interactive computing and exploration.

With the surrogate basics in place, Chap. 3 presents the sparse grid method in its classical version. Our focus will be on interpolation and the decisive feature of sparse grids, namely their hierarchical and incremental structure. Fully adaptive sparse grids are used in the sense that new interpolation points are added to an existing surrogate to improve the local or overall accuracy.

Chapter 4 reviews the most relevant computational steering environments and methods. We will see that the high-fidelity model has usually been the central aspect of most steering approaches. Other approaches combine different resolutions of the same simulation to get closer to interactivity. By extending the classical methods with surrogates, we argue that the exploration workflow is significantly improved.

The main contribution of this work is laid out in Chap. 5 where sparse grids are formulated as surrogate models. The hierarchical coefficients are used to provide additional insight with respect to changes in the behavior of the simulation. A set of visual analytics tools are adapted to guide the user to regions of interest. Thus, the surrogate does not only deliver fast solutions, but also offers exploration indicators. On the intrusive track, we develop the localized DEIM as a significant improvement to the classical DEIM for problems with separable non-linearities.

The technical realization of the distributed and parallel surrogate models is presented in Chap. 6. The notion *Repository* will be an abstraction describing a system with a slim interface that delivers new snapshots to a visualization client. GPU, CPU and hybrid repository implementations are formulated and evaluated regarding performance.

Chapter 7 demonstrates the applicability of the proposed methods to our set of four applications. Each application is described with respect to the overall setup, number and type of parameters, discretization, output of interest, and specific challenging aspects. For each high-fidelity model the corresponding surrogate is discussed and the insight indicators are checked against the known behavior. Finally, we end with concluding remarks in Chap. 8.

The main question now is, can surrogates provide fast insight? The next chapters will provide a detailed answer.

2 TECHNIQUES FOR REDUCING THE COMPLEXITY OF SIMULATIONS

2.1 SURROGATES FOR COMPUTATIONAL SIMULATIONS

The field of supercomputing follows the trend to ever larger simulations on tera-, peta- or even exascale. Thought as capability computing, a supercomputer aims to use the maximum computing power to solve a single large problem in the shortest amount of time.

In contrast, capacity computing is typically thought of as using efficiently cost-effective computing power to solve a small number of somewhat large problems or a large number of small problems. Many engineering applications fall in this second category where a filtering of relevant simulation scenarios or an investigation of parameter sensitivity will need a potentially large number of computationally intensive runs with different start parameters. Working with the high-fidelity model becomes prohibitive, if the total execution time of the number of simulations needed to reach to goal overshoots the overall time allocated for this task.

Figure 2 points out two possible ways to reduce the execution time of a costly simulation. Unlike common speedup techniques, surrogates take a different approach. The speedup in fulfilling a task (e.g, optimization, what-if analysis) is not obtained by parallelism, but by reducing the *frequency* or *cost* of high-fidelity evaluations.

The frequency of high-fidelity model evaluations can be reduced by using approximations to the input-output relationship. In many cases the output is an aggregated quantity (e.g. average temperature over entire domain) and tends to have a much smoother behavior (response) than the highly non-linear simulation itself.

A reduction in cost is achieved by taking advantage of data redundancy. Intuitively, a set of simulation snapshots can be seen as a set of observations of possibly correlated variables. Through an orthogonal transformation this set can be converted into a set of values of linearly uncorrelated variables called principal components V (see 2.5 for the computation). Suppose X be a matrix whose columns are

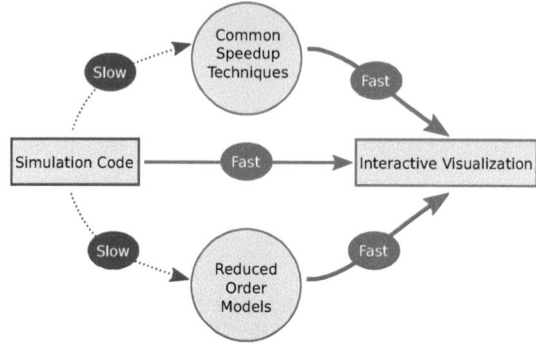

Figure 2: A slow simulation can be made interactive with common speedup techniques: parallelization or more powerful hardware. The second option is to reduce the complexity of the high-fidelity model.

given by two snapshots each with four elements. X can be expressed with the help of its principal components as follows:

$$\underbrace{\begin{bmatrix} 1 & 2.2 \\ 2 & 4.1 \\ 4 & 8.1 \\ 8 & 16.3 \end{bmatrix}}_{X} = \underbrace{\begin{bmatrix} -0.1154 & 0.9440 \\ -0.2180 & 0.1422 \\ -0.4317 & -0.2976 \\ -0.8676 & -0.0132 \end{bmatrix}}_{V} \times \underbrace{\begin{bmatrix} -9.2193 & -18.7869 \\ -0.0680 & 0.0334 \end{bmatrix}}_{X_r} \quad (1)$$

Thus, with no loss of information, any linear operations done on X can also be done on X_r where $X_r = V^T X$. The difference is that X_r is significantly smaller. After performing computations with the lower-dimensional X_r the return to the high-dimensional space is done with VX_r. Significant computational reduction is achieved in solving a linear PDE by using the low-dimensional X_r instead of X.

2.2 CLASSIFICATION OF SURROGATE MODELS

Three main categories of surrogates can be distinguished by the way the reduction in cost is pursued [31].

Hierarchical surrogates are physics-based models in the sense that PDE are still simulated but in a lower fidelity version. Typical simplifications are the use of coarser discretizations, weaker convergence tolerances, or simpler physics. From the computational steering point of view, approaches using hierarchical surrogates have been actively pursued (see [54]). The idea is that a sufficiently coarse discretization delivers results at interactive rates. Difficulties might arise when a too low discretization does not capture simulation behavior which would be relevant for the understanding of the simulation.

Reduced-order modeling techniques such as proper orthogonal decomposition in computational fluid dynamics or modal analysis in structural dynamics also have physics linkage. They solve the PDE system, but projected on the most important modes of the state space. Orders of magnitude for the reduction can be achieved, if the system behavior is represented with only very few modes. Their derivation for a new problem tends to require significant effort, but the achieved accuracy makes them some of the most successful surrogates.

Data fit surrogates are non-physics-based approximations typically involving interpolation or regression of a set of data generated from the high-fidelity model. Within data fit models we will focus on the ones which offer a global approximation. Such techniques [48] deliver low-fidelity results over the entire parameter space, which is needed by a global exploration approach. Some prominent members of this category are *polynomial response surfaces*, stochastic collocation, *Kriging* [50], *neural networks, radial basis functions* [69], or *spline interpolation*.

A further classification of surrogate models is based on the amount of work needed to construct the surrogate model for a new simulation. Reduced order surrogates require a transformation of the original PDE and thus fall in the category of *intrusive* methods while data fit surrogates are *non-intrusive* as only the quantity to be interpolated or approximated changes.

We will next elaborate on the fundamental concept of a surrogate and proceed with some intrusive and non-intrusive methods. The chapter closes with an evaluation of their suitability in an interactive computational steering setting.

2.3 OFFLINE - ONLINE PATTERN

A surrogate model is used instead of the simulation to enable fast evaluation, obtaining approximate solutions significantly faster than running the original simulation. This is achieved by investing computational effort in building the surrogate model *offline*, which can then be evaluated very fast during the actual *online* steering. In this work, let us denote with $\mathbf{u}(\mathbf{x}, \boldsymbol{\mu})$, $\mathbf{u} : \Omega \times \mathcal{P} \to \mathbb{R}^N$, the simulation function we seek to approximate, which depends on the physical 2- or 3-dimensional coordinates $\mathbf{x} \in \Omega$ and the vector $\boldsymbol{\mu} \in \mathcal{P}$ of normalized d parameters, where

$$\mathcal{P} = \{\boldsymbol{\mu} \mid \boldsymbol{\mu} \in (0,1)^d , \ d \geqslant 1\} \qquad (2)$$

8 TECHNIQUES FOR REDUCING THE COMPLEXITY OF SIMULATIONS

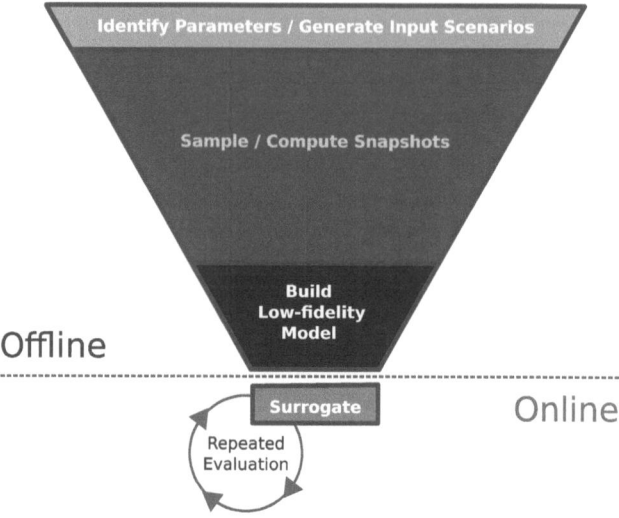

Figure 3: The two phases of the surrogate process: offline and online. For a particular simulation scenario the relevant parameters and their ranges are fixed. For each sample point in $\mathcal{P}_s$, the corresponding simulation is computed. Usually, this is the most time-consuming part of the offline phase. The low-fidelity model is built from the precomputed snapshots. Online, this cheaper model is used in an evaluation loop.

is the relevant parameter space for the simulation. For a fixed μ the simulation instance is called a snapshot $\mathbf{u}^\mu(\mathbf{x}) := \mathbf{u}(\mathbf{x}, \mu)$ and represents the result of the simulation started with μ as parameter values. For reasons of simplicity, $\mathbf{u}^\mu$ will be used to denote the entire 2- or 3-dimensional simulation snapshot corresponding to μ. The output of the surrogate model $\tilde{\mathbf{u}}(\mathbf{x}, \mu)$ is also called a snapshot and will be denoted $\tilde{\mathbf{u}}^\mu(\mathbf{x}) := \tilde{\mathbf{u}}(\mathbf{x}, \mu)$, or simply $\tilde{\mathbf{u}}^\mu$ for the full surrogate solution.

Figure 3 illustrates the main parts of a surrogate model approach. The construction of the surrogate model is done offline and starts by choosing the parameters and their ranges of interest. This is simulation specific, but is also limited by the amount of effort worth investing in the offline phase, as a larger parameter count and range, while desirable, will increase the cost of the offline phase. Next, a sampling is performed within the chosen ranges and for each parameter combination a full simulation is performed and stored. We will denote the set of sampling points $\mathcal{P}_s \subset \mathcal{P}$. A necessary condition is that the sampling covers a large part of the informational content and behavior of the simulation itself.

For the chosen sampling $\mathcal{P}_s$ all the corresponding simulation snapshots are computed. The offline phase ends with a surrogate-model-specific reduction technique, which constructs for the original problem $\mathbf{u}$ the reduced form $\tilde{\mathbf{u}}$, with $\tilde{\mathbf{u}}$ being more suitable for fast repeated evaluation. The actual exploration takes place in the online phase using $\tilde{\mathbf{u}}$, where the user can frequently change parameters, and, guided by an interactive visualization, study the behavior of the original simulation.

2.4 NON-INTRUSIVE SURROGATE MODELS

Non-intrusive approaches treat the high-fidelity model as a black box out of which the sampling $\mathcal{P}_s$ is drawn. A new snapshot is constructed as a sum of weighted basis functions where one of the two things is to be computed: (1) the weights (Kriging, polynomial chaos, radial basis functions) or (2) the basis functions (stochastic collocation).

2.4.1 *Kriging*

Kriging [40, 83, 51, 46] belongs to the family of least squares estimation algorithms. The aim of Kriging is to estimate the value of an unknown real-valued function $u(\mu)$ at point μ given some observations at points $\mu_1, \ldots, \mu_M$. A Kriging estimator is said to be linear because the predicted value $\tilde{u}^\mu$ is a linear combination that may be written as

$$\tilde{u}(\mu) = \sum_{i=1}^{M} \alpha_i(\mu) u(\mu_i) \qquad (3)$$

where the weights α_i must be chosen to satisfy that $\tilde{u}$: (1) is unbiased and (2) optimal with respect to the minimum squared error. These conditions are then expressed as the constrained optimization problem:

$$\begin{aligned} E[u(\mu) - \tilde{u}(\mu)] &= 0 & (4)\\ Var[u(\mu) - \tilde{u}(\mu)] \text{ is } & \text{ minimum} & (5) \end{aligned}$$

The most common type of Kriging is ordinary Kriging which assumes an unknown but constant mean, $E[u] = \bar{u}$, and requires enough observations to construct the semivariogram

$$\gamma(\mu_i, \mu_j) = E[(u(\mu_i) - u(\mu_j))^2]. \qquad (6)$$

The semivariogram describes the degree of spatial dependence and thus correlation between the available function evaluations $u(\mu_1)$, ..., $u(\mu_M)$. If there is spatial dependence, values that are closer together (in the parameter space) will have small variance and vice versa. As $u(\mu)$ is only known at the sampling points but the semivariogram is needed at all interpolation points, the empirical semivariogram is used:

$$\hat{\gamma}(\mu_1, \mu_2) = \hat{\gamma}(\mu_1 - \mu_2) = \hat{\gamma}(h) = \frac{1}{|D(h)|} \sum_{(i,j) \in D(h)} |u(\mu_i) - u(\mu_j)|^2 \qquad (7)$$

where $D(h)$ denotes the set of pairs of snapshots i, j corresponding to a parameter distance $|\mu_i - \mu_j| = h$, and $|D(h)|$ is the number of pairs in the set. Based on the semivariogram, for a new parameter μ^* the following Kriging system is solved:

$$\begin{pmatrix} \alpha_1 \\ \vdots \\ \alpha_M \\ \sigma \end{pmatrix} = \underbrace{\begin{pmatrix} \gamma(\mu_1, \mu_1) & \cdots & \gamma(\mu_1, \mu_M) & 1 \\ \vdots & \ddots & \vdots & \vdots \\ \gamma(\mu_M, \mu_1) & \cdots & \gamma(\mu_M, \mu_M) & 1 \\ 1 & \cdots & 1 & 0 \end{pmatrix}^{-1}}_{\text{offline}} \underbrace{\begin{pmatrix} \gamma(\mu_1, \mu^*) \\ \vdots \\ \gamma(\mu_M, \mu^*) \\ 1 \end{pmatrix}}_{\text{online}} \qquad (8)$$

where σ is a Lagrange multiplier used to ensure the unbiasedness condition. The interpolation by ordinary Kriging is then done online with

$$\tilde{u}(\mu^*) = \underbrace{\begin{pmatrix} \alpha_1 \\ \vdots \\ \alpha_M \end{pmatrix}'}_{\text{computed}} \underbrace{\begin{pmatrix} u(\mu_1) \\ \vdots \\ u(\mu_M) \end{pmatrix}}_{\text{stored}} \qquad (9)$$

The above equations describe Kriging for a function of one variable. When interpolating a field of size N the costs scale linearly. In order to perform the linear sum in Eq. 3 the Kriging coefficients α_i need to be computed online (at interpolation time). N sets of coefficients are computed, one for each discretization node in the snapshot. While the matrix inverse in Eq. 8 is precomputed, we still need to perform N matrix vector products of size M at interpolation time. Furthermore, in oder to improve the estimator with additional observations all precomputed matrix inverses in Eq. 8 need to be recomputed.

2.4.2 Non-Intrusive Polynomial Chaos

Polynomial Chaos (PC) has been successfully used in uncertainty quantification [29, 30, 43] to compute how uncertainties in the input of a dynamical system manifest in its outputs. It relies on orthogonal polynomials to construct a response $\tilde{u}$ to the parameters μ given their known input probability distribution function $\rho(\mu)$. The output is thus expressed as the series:

$$\tilde{u}(\mu^*) = \alpha(\mu_0)P_0(\mu^*) + \alpha(\mu_1)P_1(\mu^*) + \alpha(\mu_2)P_2(\mu^*) + \ldots \quad (10)$$

The orthogonal polynomials P_k are related to ρ by:

$$\int P_j(\mu)P_k(\mu)\rho(\mu)d\mu = \delta_{j,k} \quad (11)$$

To unknown coefficients α_k can be computed by intrusive [97, 98] or non-intrusive methods. The later can be regression [7, 90] or projection [89, 18] based. The projection method takes advantage of the orthogonality properties of the PC representation and computes the expansion coefficients from some evaluations of the high-fidelity model u:

$$\alpha_k = \frac{1}{N_k} \int u(\mu)P(\mu)\rho(\mu)d\mu \quad (12)$$

$$\alpha_k \approx \frac{1}{N_k} \sum_{i=1}^{M} u(\mu_i)P_k(\mu_i)w_i \quad (13)$$

$$N_k = \int P_k^2(\mu)\rho(\mu)d\mu \quad (14)$$

where $u(\mu_i), i = 1\ldots M$ are, as with Kriging, M precomputed snapshots for different values of μ sampled according to $\rho(\mu)$.

When used as a surrogate in a steering context, the input parameters are uniformly distributed and the Legendre polynomials are the best choice for P_i (see [29]). The quadrature in Eq. 13 is the main computational cost but takes place offline. Similar to Kriging, any extension of the surrogate requires quadrature computations and makes is problematic for on-the-fly improvement.

2.4.3 Stochastic Collocation

Collocation methods [30, 57] construct an interpolant to the response u under the condition that the surrogate coincides (is collocated), $\widetilde{u}(\mu_i) = u(\mu_i)$, at the sampling points $\mu_i, i = 1\ldots M$. The Stochastic Collocation (SC) expansion is usually formed as a sum of multidimensional Lagrange interpolation polynomials of degree $M - 1$. The coefficients of the expansion are just the response values at each of the collocation points. Unlike PC, which constructs coefficients to known polynomials, SC builds polynomials to known coefficients:

$$u \approx \widetilde{u} = \sum_{j=1}^{M} u(\mu_j) L_j(\mu) \qquad (15)$$

$$L_j = \prod_{k=1, k\neq j}^{M} \frac{\mu - \mu_k}{\mu_j - \mu_k} \qquad (16)$$

where M is the size of the set of collocated points. In the uncertainty quantification scenario the solution has to be integrated, thus Gauss points are used as collocation points. With an increasing number of dimensions the quadrature runs into the curse of dimensionality and sparse grid quadrature is typically used.

Having global support, the evaluation of the interpolant requires all snapshots. This poses efficiency challenges in the context of interactive results. Furthermore, any extension to the model adds new support points and thus requires rebuilding the polynomials.

2.5 INTRUSIVE SURROGATE MODELS

Intrusive reduction methods do not treat the simulation as a black box but instead solve the initial system of PDEs in a significantly reduced space. A popular reduction method is the Proper Orthogonal Decomposition (POD) [77, 42, 87]. Depending on the field of application it is also known as the discrete Karhunen–Loève expansion or principal components analysis (PCA). For a given set of simulation snapshots $x_1, x_2, \ldots, x_M \in \mathbb{R}^N$, where $x_i = \mathbf{u}(\mu_i)$ is the snapshot for the parameter μ_i, POD computes a set of orthogonal vectors $V_1, V_2, \ldots, V_M \in \mathbb{R}^{N \times 1}$ that capture the dominant structure of X (see

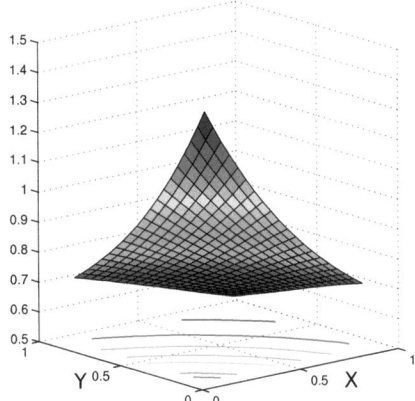

Figure 4: The one peak function
$$u(\mu) = \frac{1.0}{\sqrt{(x-\mu(1)-0.1)^2+(y-\mu(2)-0.1)^2+0.1^2}}.$$

Fig. 4 and 5 for an example). Once available, each snapshot x_i can be expressed as a linear combination of V_i:

$$x_i = \underbrace{\begin{bmatrix} | & & | \\ V_1 & \cdots & V_M \\ | & & | \end{bmatrix}}_{V} \begin{bmatrix} | \\ c_i \\ | \end{bmatrix} = Vc_i \qquad (17)$$

where $c_i \in \mathbb{R}^{M \times 1}$ are coefficients of the linear combination. The most important properties of V are their orthogonality and their decreasing contribution to the linear representation of x_i (V_1 is the most important mode while V_M the least important). This means that for a given $k \leqslant M$, POD generates a set of orthonormal vectors of dimension k $(V_1, \ldots, V_k)$, which minimize the approximation error:

$$\min_{\{V_i\}_{i=1}^k} \sum_{j=1}^{M} \|x_j - \hat{x}_j\|^2, \qquad (18)$$

where $\hat{x}_j = \sum_{i=1}^k \overbrace{\langle x_j, V_i \rangle}^{c_i} V_i$ is an approximation of x_j using only $\{V_i\}_{i=1}^k$. It turns out that the solution of the above minimization prob-

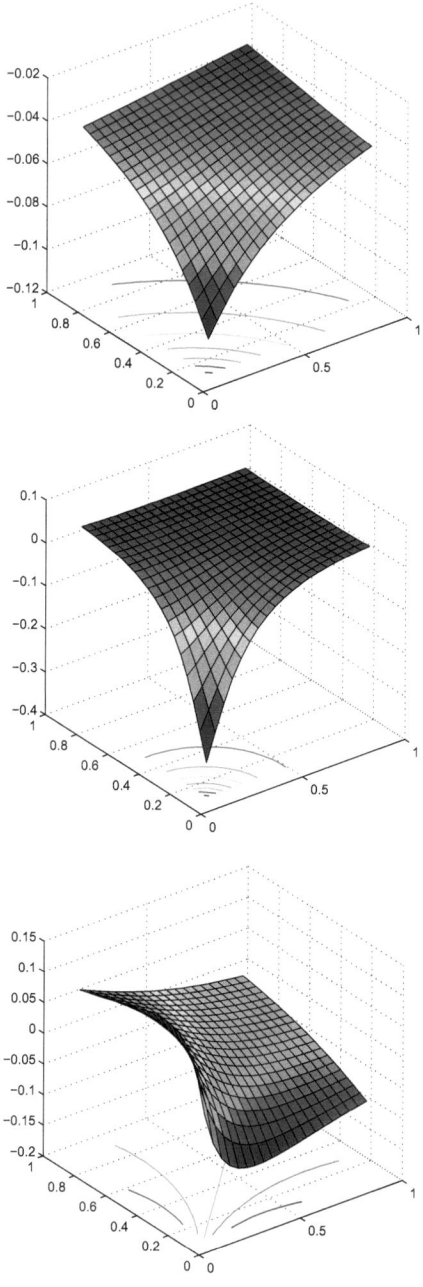

Figure 5: The first 3 modes (top to bottom) used to approximate the one peak function u.

lem is given by the *Singular Value Decomposition* (SVD, [37]) of the snapshot matrix X:

$$X = \begin{bmatrix} | & & | \\ x_1 & \cdots & x_M \\ | & & | \end{bmatrix} \in \mathbb{R}^{N \times M} \qquad (19)$$

The searched V_i are the left-singular vectors from $SVD(X) = V\Sigma W^T$. The singular values on the diagonal of Σ give the magnitude of importance of the corresponding singular vector, thus, the selection of k is usually done by setting a prescribed energy content to be captured by the first k left-singular vectors (e.g 90%):

$$\frac{\sum_{i=1}^{k} \lambda_i}{\sum_{i=1}^{M} \lambda_i} \geqslant 0.9 \qquad (20)$$

2.5.1 Reduction of a Linear System

Besides its use in image processing [81], data compression or signal analysis [1], the POD method plays a central role in the reduction of differential equation systems [66, 42]. The aim is to reduce the initial equation system of size N to one of much smaller size k. We illustrate the procedure with the linear time-dependent ODE:

$$\dot{x}(t) = Ax(t) \qquad (21)$$
$$x^0 = x(0) \qquad (22)$$

The state $x : [0, T] \to \mathbb{R}^N$ consists of all degrees of freedom in the simulation domain, while $A \in \mathbb{R}^{N \times N}$ stems (e.g) from a finite difference discretization of a large linear PDE. After computing the SVD of the snapshot matrix we choose only $k \ll N$ columns from $V = \{V_1, \ldots, V_k\}$. The system is reduced with the substitution $x(t) \to V x_r(t)$, $V \in \mathbb{R}^{N \times k}$, $x_r(t) \in \mathbb{R}^{k \times 1}$:

$$V^T V \dot{x}_r(t) \stackrel{(V^T *)}{=} V^T A V x_r(t)$$
$$\underbrace{\dot{x}_r(t)}_{k \times 1} = \underbrace{A_r}_{k \times k} \underbrace{x_r(t)}_{k \times 1}$$

The resulting system has no more dependence on the very large N.

2.5.2 Reduction of a Non-Linear System

For a linear system, the previous reduction is quite straightforward. More complex is the reduction of a non-linear system of the form

$$\dot{x}(t) = Ax(t) + F(x(t)) \qquad (23)$$
$$x^0 = x(0) \qquad (24)$$

where $F = [f(x_1(t)), \ldots, f(x_N(t))]^T$ is the non-linear term obtained by evaluating the expensive non-linear function $f : \mathbb{R} \to \mathbb{R}$ at the components of $x(t)$. With a choice of $k \ll N$ we can proceed with the reduction as in the linear case with the substitution $x(t) \to Vx_r(t)$, $V \in \mathbb{R}^{N \times k}$, $x_r(t) \in \mathbb{R}^{k \times 1}$:

$$V^T V \dot{x}_r(t) \stackrel{(V^T*)}{=} V^T A V x_r(t) + V^T F(V x_r(t)) \qquad (25)$$
$$\underbrace{\dot{x}_r(t)}_{k \times 1} = \underbrace{A_r}_{k \times k} \underbrace{x_r(t)}_{k \times 1} + \underbrace{V^T}_{k \times N} \underbrace{F(V x_r(t))}_{N \times 1} \qquad (26)$$

However, in the non-linear system there is still dependence on the very large N which makes the straightforward reduction unfeasible. To reduce also the non-linear term we give an overview of the Discrete Empirical Interpolation Method (DEIM) [15, 14, 16] which extends the POD method. DEIM approximates $f(t) := F(Vx_r(t))$ with the help of another set of orthogonal vectors $U \in \mathbb{R}^{N \times M}$ with $M \ll N$ and coefficients $c(t)$:

$$f(t) \approx U c(t) \qquad (27)$$

The approximation then becomes:

$$V^T \hat{F}(x(t)) = V^T f(t) \approx \underbrace{V^T U}_{\text{precomp}: k \times M} \underbrace{c(t)}_{M \times 1} \qquad (28)$$

Independence of the very large N is obtained provided that the unknown $c(t)$ can be computed. To obtain an expression for $c(t)$ first assume $f(t)$ is entirely available. In that case the system of equations from 27 is overdetermined with $M \ll N$. To make the system determined, we need to extract only M lines of $f(t)$ and U (with the row extraction matrix P^T), a relation for $c(t)$ is deduced:

$$P^T f(t) = (P^T U) c(t)$$
$$c(t) = \underbrace{(P^T U)^{-1}}_{\text{precomp}} P^T f(t)$$

Thus, in order to compute $c(t)$ only m evaluations of the nonlinear term $f(t)$ are needed. By putting everything together:

$$\widehat{f}(t) = Uc(t) \quad = \quad U(P^T U)^{-1} P^T f(t) \qquad (29)$$

$$V^T \widehat{f}(t) \quad \stackrel{(V^T *)}{=} \quad V^T U(P^T U)^{-1} P^T f(t) \qquad (30)$$

$$\underbrace{V^T F(V x_r(t))}_{n \times 1} \quad \stackrel{f(t):=F(V x_r(t))}{\approx} \quad \underbrace{\underbrace{V^T U(P^T U)^{-1}}_{\text{precomp: } k \times m} \underbrace{F(P^T V x_r(t))}_{m \times 1}}_{\text{reduced non linear term}} \qquad (31)$$

There is still the decision of which lines should the extraction operator P^T choose. DEIM employs the following heuristic algorithm:

Algorithm 1 DEIM

Input: $U = \{u_1, u_2, \ldots, u_m\}$, from SVD of nonlinear snapshots
Output: $\vec{P} = \{P_1, P_2, \ldots, P_m\}$
$P_1 \leftarrow \vec{0}$
$i \leftarrow \arg\max_i |u_1[i]|$
$P_1[i] \leftarrow 1$
$U \leftarrow [u_1]$
$\vec{P} \leftarrow [P_1]$
for $j = 2$ to m **do**
  $u \leftarrow u_j$
  $c \leftarrow U_{\vec{P}}^T u_{\vec{P}}$
  $r \leftarrow u - Uc$
  $i \leftarrow \arg\max_i |r_1[i]|$
  $P_j \leftarrow \vec{0}$
  $P_j[i] \leftarrow 1$
  $U \leftarrow [U\ u],\ \vec{P} \leftarrow \begin{bmatrix} \vec{P} & P_j \end{bmatrix}$
end for

, where $\{P_1, P_2, \ldots, P_m\}$ are vectors with one at the position of the node to be selected and zero elsewhere.

For the "one peak" function in Fig. 4 DEIM does a good job at choosing DEIM points, which are representative for the non-linearity (see Fig. 6).

2.6 SUMMARY

Intrusive and non-intrusive surrogate models both aim to reduce the computation cost of the high-fidelity simulations so that fast repeated evaluation (simulation) is possible. Any of these methods is able to deliver low-fidelity snapshots. However, what is needed for interactive computational steering is close to real-time result delivery and also

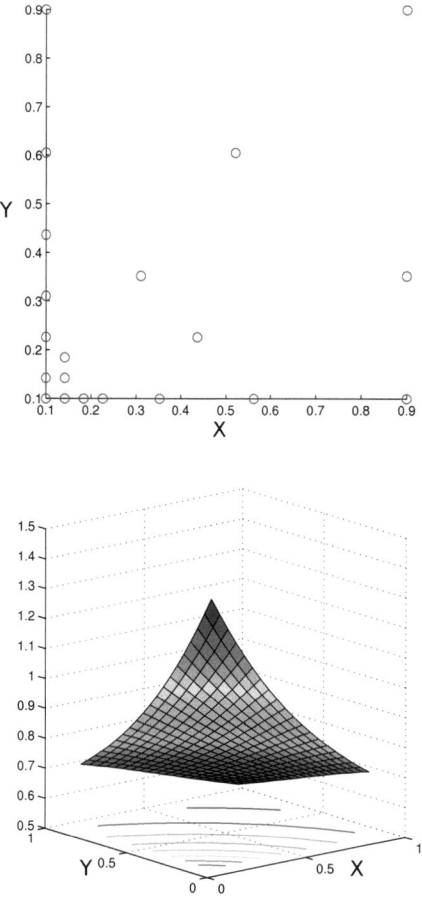

Figure 6: DEIM points (top) for the one peak function (bottom). More DEIM points are invested for the approximation of the function peak towards $\mu = (0.1, 0.1)$.

extensibility of the model at user request. These two requirements pose difficulties to the presented methods and invite us to search for alternative surrogates. The next chapter deals with sparse grid interpolation. With a proper formulation and efficient implementation, this method fulfills both requirements and is thus suited to support interactive computational steering.

3

REDUCING COMPLEXITY WITH SPARSE GRIDS

The curse of dimensionality is an infamous phenomena that arises when analyzing and organizing data in high-dimensional spaces. It can be understood as the exponential increase in effort associated with adding extra dimensions to a problem space. For example, moving from a 2-dimensional discretization of size N^2 to a 3-dimensional grid increases the storage requirements but also the complexity of a CFD solver by a factor of N. With sufficiently large dimensionality d any problem becomes intractable on the resulting grid (N^d) and special approaches to reducing complexity are needed.

An example of such a problem is interpolation. Interpolation is a method to construct new data points within the range of a discrete set of known data points, usually laid on a grid or in a structured manner. For *univariate* interpolation several types of methods are well established: *linear* interpolation, *spline* interpolation, *polynomial* interpolation and *radial basis* interpolation. Additional forms of interpolation can be constructed by choosing a different class of interpolants: *rational* functions, *trigonometric* polynomials, or *wavelets*.

Central to this work, *multivariate* interpolation is the interpolation of functions of more than one variable and includes bilinear and bicubic interpolation in two dimensions, and tri-linear interpolation in three dimensions. Several univariate interpolation methods can be extend beyond three dimensions by using tensor product approaches. However, for many approaches the fact remains that if there are N terms in the 1-dimensional interpolation formula, then there will be N^d terms in the d-dimensional case.

3.1 SPARSE GRIDS IN A NUTSHELL

Sparse grids help to overcome the curse of dimensionality to a great extent. Interpolating a d-dimensional function u on a regular grid with a resolution of N grid points in each dimension, they enable one to reduce the number of grid points significantly from $\mathcal{O}(N^d)$ to $\mathcal{O}(N(\log N)^{d-1})$, while maintaining a similar accuracy as in the full grid case—at least if u is sufficiently smooth [10]. The notion *sparse grids* was coined in 1990 for the solution of high-dimensional partial differential equations (PDEs) [99], and they have meanwhile been successfully employed in a whole range of applications, ranging from astrophysics and quantum chemistry to data mining and computational finance, see, e.g., [10, 75] and the references cited there. In the following, we briefly describe sparse grids and the main principles they base upon, a hierarchical representation of the one-dimensional basis and the extension to the d-dimensional setting via a tensor product approach. For further details, we refer to [10].

We consider the representation of a piecewise d-linear function $\tilde{u} : \Omega \to \Gamma$ for a certain mesh-width $h_n := 2^{-n}$ with some discretization level n. We consider rectangular domains Ω which we scale to $\Omega := [0, 1]^d$. To obtain an interpolant $\tilde{u}$ as an approximation to some function u, we discretize Ω and employ basis functions ϕ_i which are centered at the grid points stemming from the discretization. $\tilde{u}$ is thus a weighted sum of N basis functions, $\tilde{u} := \sum_{j=1}^{N} \alpha_j \phi_j$, with coefficients α_j.

The underlying principle is a hierarchical formulation of the basis functions. In one dimension, we use the standard hierarchical basis

$$\Phi_l := \left\{ \varphi_{l',i} : l' \leqslant l, i \leqslant 2^{l'} - 1 \wedge i \text{ odd} \right\}.$$

with piecewise linear ansatz functions $\varphi_{l,i}(\mu) := \varphi\left(\mu \cdot 2^l - i\right)$ and $\varphi(\mu) := \max(1 - |\mu|, 0)$ for some level $l \geqslant 1$ and an index $1 \leqslant i < 2^l$. The basis functions are centered at grid points $\mu_{l,i} = 2^{-l}i$ at which we interpolate u, see Fig. 7 (left) for the basis functions up to level 3. Note that all basis functions on one level have pairwise disjoint supports and cover the whole domain.

The hierarchical basis functions can be extended to d dimensions via a tensor product approach as

$$\varphi_{\underline{l},\underline{i}}(\mu) := \prod_{j=1}^{d} \varphi_{l_j, i_j}(\mu_j),$$

with multi-indices $\underline{l}$ and $\underline{i}$ indicating level and index of the underlying one-dimensional hat functions for each dimension. The d-dimensional basis

$$\Phi_{W_{\underline{l}}} := \left\{ \varphi_{\underline{l},\underline{i}}(\mu) : i_j = 1, \ldots, 2^{l_j} - 1, i_j \text{ odd}, 1 \leqslant j \leqslant d \right\}$$

span hierarchical subspaces $W_{\underline{l}}$. As before, the basis functions for each $W_{\underline{l}}$ have pairwise disjoint, equally sized supports and cover the whole domain. The classical full-grid space of piecewise d-linear functions V_n can be obtained as a direct sum of $W_{\underline{l}}$,

$$V_n := \sum_{l_1=1}^{n} \cdots \sum_{l_d=1}^{n} W_{(l_1,\ldots,l_d)} = \bigoplus_{|\underline{l}|_\infty \leqslant n} W_{\underline{l}},$$

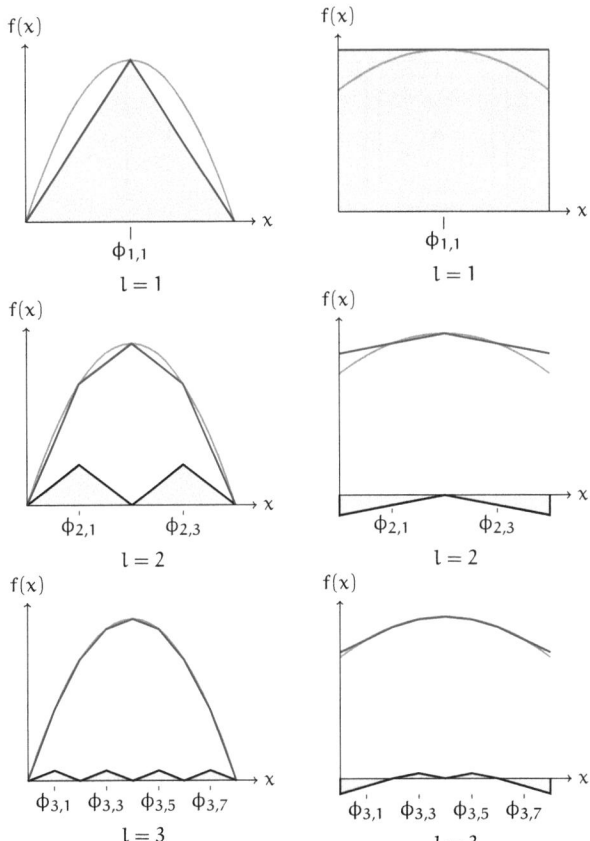

Figure 7: Left: classical one-dimensional hierarchical basis functions (grey-filled) up to level 3. The orange line is an example function to be interpolated. The interpolant (blue line) is the weighted sum of hierarchical bases (grey-filled triangles) from the current and all previous levels. Right: modified extrapolating basis functions. On $l = 1$ the basis function is constant, while all other levels have the basis functions at the far left and far right flipped to extrapolate towards the boundary.

but the hierarchical scheme of subspaces allows one to choose those subspaces that contribute most to the approximation. By choosing

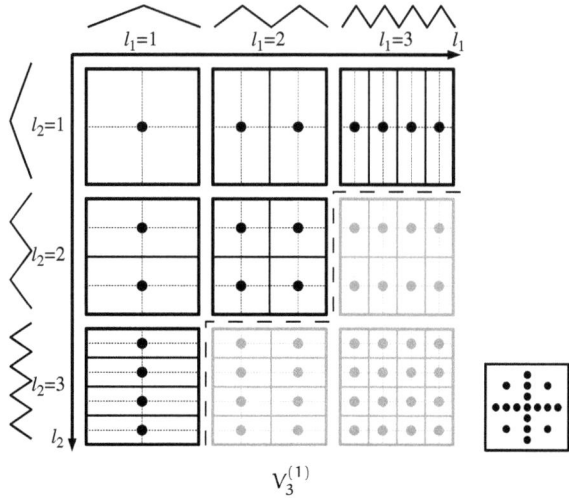

Figure 8: The tableau of subspaces $W_{\underline{l}}$ up to level 3 in two dimensions (left) together with the resulting sparse grid for $n = 3$ (right).

subspaces with respect to their contribution in the L_2-norm, this leads to the sparse grid space $V_n^{(1)}$,

$$V_n^{(1)} := \bigoplus_{|\underline{l}|_1 \leqslant n+d-1} W_{\underline{l}}.$$

The tableau of subspaces in 2D is shown in Fig. 8 for $n = 3$.

To obtain non-zero values on the boundary, the one-dimensional basis of level 1 can be extended by the two basis functions $\varphi_{0,0}$ and $\varphi_{0,1}$. Unfortunately, even for a very coarse grid with a resolution of $h_1 = 1/2$ this requires 3^d function evaluations—with $3^d - 1$ parameter combinations being located on the boundary of the parameter space Ω. For our application of computational steering, we start with a reasonable choice of Ω so that these extreme parameter combinations are of less interest compared to the inner part of Ω. We therefore choose to interpolate only in the inner part and to extrapolate towards the boundary. We use in the following the one-dimensional basis functions:

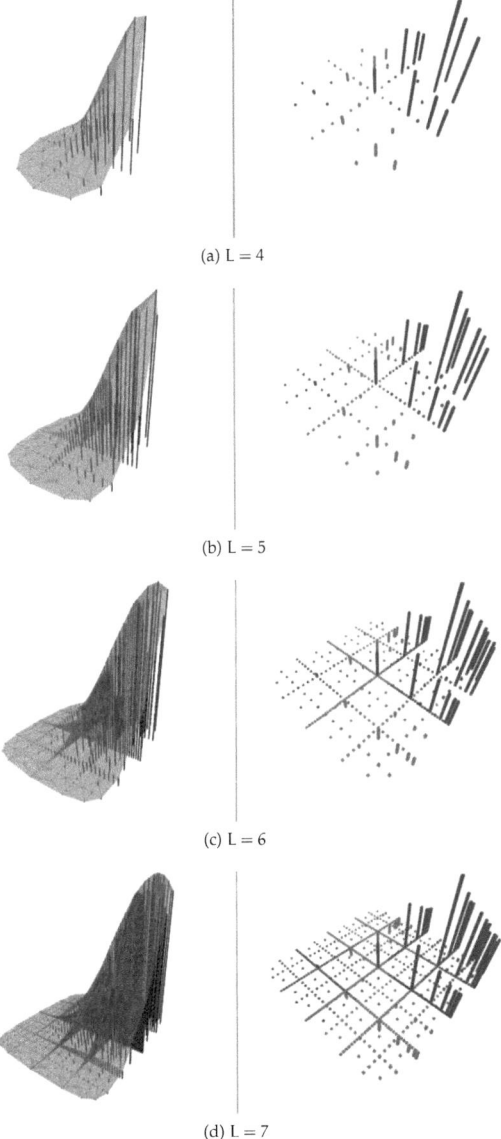

Figure 9: Left: Interpolation of a function using regular sparse grids of increasing level. Right: Corresponding hierarchical coefficients. Blue lines are positive and red are negative contributions. Notice larger coefficients where the function peaks.

$$\varphi_{l,i}(x) := \begin{cases} 1 & \text{if } l = 1 \wedge i = 1, \\ \begin{cases} 2 - 2^l \cdot x & \text{if } x \in [0, \frac{1}{2^{l-1}}] \\ 0 & \text{else} \end{cases} & \text{if } l > 1 \wedge i = 1, \\ \begin{cases} 2^l \cdot x + 1 - i & \text{if } x \in [1 - \frac{1}{2^{l-1}}, 1] \\ 0 & \text{else} \end{cases} & \text{if } l > 1 \wedge i = 2^l - 1, \\ \varphi\left(x \cdot 2^l - i\right) & \text{else} \end{cases} \quad (32)$$

depicted in Fig. 7 (right).

For a visual understanding of the interpolation process Fig. 9 (left) shows a two dimensional function discretized on an sparse grid of increasing level using linear basis functions. In Fig. 9 (right) the discretization is showed once again, but at each point a colored bar is placed. The height of the bar is given by the hierarchical coefficient at that grid point.

3.2 ADAPTIVE SPARSE GRIDS

The classical structure of the sparse grid is based a selection of points which is optimal with respect to the smoothness conditions and guarantees a priori error bounds with no additional function knowledge.

Adaptive sparse grid have been successfully used to approximate functions which do not fulfill the smoothness criteria of the classical method (see [75, 47]). Non-linearities in the form of peaks or steps can be directly targeted by spending more interpolation points in those regions.

To refine a grid point, often all 2^d children need to be added (see Fig. 10). As most algorithms use the hierarchical structure of basis functions, it must be ensured that newly added grid points can be reached starting from any dimension. In Fig. 10 a point is refined by adding its corresponding children. To complete the hierarchical structure two additional ancestors are added (see Fig. 10 right).

Stemming from the hierarchical construction, the absolute value of the hierarchical surplus reflects the contribution of a grid point to the interpolation. For many functions it is safe to assume that children (neighbors) of points with large surpluses also contribute significantly to the interpolation quality in that area. The surplus magnitude is thus the most straightforward refinement indicator, which we also successfully use on this work.

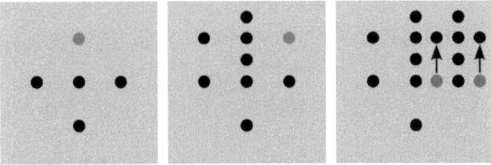

Figure 10: For a two dimensional sparse grid with $l = 2$ (left) we perform a refinement of a single point (marked with red). This implies adding the 2^d hierarchical children to the current grid (middle). A further refinement of another red-colored point adds 2^2 children but also their hierarchical ancestors in all dimensions (the two green points in this case) (right). They are necessary as most sparse grid algorithms traverse the hierarchical structure top-down (arrows indicate how the new children will be visited in the vertical dimension).

At any time, all points on the last hierarchical level can be considered for refinement. For functions where a single evaluation is very expensive a decision needs to be made regarding the purpose of the refinement. If function jumps need to be well captured, then local refinement in the vicinity of the jump is employed. However, when interested in an overall good accuracy, then care needs to be taken to avoid refinement concentrations only at discontinuities.

4 INSIGHT THROUGH INTERACTIVE COMPUTATIONAL STEERING

4.1 CLASSICAL STEERING APPROACHES

"Scientists not only want to analyze data that result from their supercomputations; they also want to interpret what is happening to the data during super-computations. Researchers want to steer calculations in close to realtime; they want to be able to change parameters, resolution or presentation, and see the effects. They want to drive the scientific discovery process; they want to interact with their data." McCormick et al.[63]

"Computational steering can be applied to good effect in a variety of computational disciplines. By monitoring the progress of simulations, aided by on-line visualization, the computational scientist avoids losing cycles to redundant computation or even doing the wrong calculation. By tuning the value of steerable parameters, the computational scientist quickly learns how the simulation responds to perturbations and can use this insight to design subsequent computational experiments." Mulder et al.[67]

"Interaction with the computational model and the resulting graphics display is fundamental in scientific visualization. Steering enhances productivity by greatly reducing the time between changes to model parameters and the viewing of the results." Marshall et al.[58]

Introduced by the above citations, computational steering is usually seen as a set of tools that supports the understanding of a simulation scenario through easy manipulation of parameters and instant delivery of corresponding solutions. In broader terms it offers a fast *mapping* between the various parameter combinations and the corresponding solution space (Fig. 11) which have one of the following two goals.

The first goal is to freely explore the parameter space. An exploration process corresponds to following a trajectory in the parameter space. Along this trajectory simulation snapshots for different parameter combinations are visually inspected and compared for interesting behavior. Such behavior is usually associated with areas of significant function change. Thus, as a point of view, freely exploring the parameter space corresponds to performing visual sensitivity analysis.

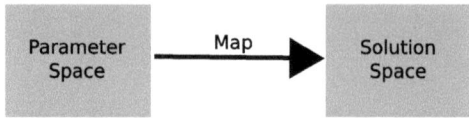

Figure 11: A more general approach to computational steering as a map from parameters to appropriate solutions.

The second main use for computational steering is to localize a particular solution or solution set which is desirable and do so in an efficient manner. Based on established search criteria, the user narrows the search down to smaller subregions in the parameter space. Plugged into an optimization process, only user-identified subregions are considered for algorithmic optimization. Such a *human-in-the-loop* process can significantly speed up the optimization of complex computationally expensive simulations.

Computational steering has usually been defined as interaction with the high-fidelity model itself: *"Computational steering refers to the real-time interaction of a scientist with their running simulation code."* Pickles et al. [76]. Before arguing that this definition can be extended to include an approximation layer based on pre-computed data, we touch on approaches to the design and implementation of computational steerings systems.

One option is to build a wrapper around a single, pre-existing specific application. This requires a means of communication between the running application and the steering client, the awareness of the application to the steering parameters, and a communication protocol for the client steering commands. The wrappers are typically developed and maintained by the application authors themselves and adapted as the code evolves. Such approaches tend to be rather specific.

A second option is the development of dedicated steering frameworks or libraries that handle in a unified way one or more central aspects to steering: communication, simulation control, data management, visualization or parallelization. Some examples are CSE [92], CUMULVUS [35] (data management), Magellan [95] (steering language) or ESPN [79] (steering of coupled codes). More recent designs such as ICARUS [8], Paraview's CoProccesing [32] or VISIT [27], focus most on in-situ visualization with steering functionality.

Another approach is to embed the application as a component within a more general problem solving environment (PSE) such as the classical SCIRun framework [74, 49] or the Cactus Framework[39]. Such environments already include parallelization, access to computational grid tools, check-pointing, multiple input/output mechanisms, and visualization. In such environments steering is achieved by setting up a workflow of user-configurable components. These comprehensive tools for interacting with an application also tend to require a significant amount of work to implement the component interface.

Furthermore, computational steering approaches such as the RealityGrid [76] aim to use the vast computational resources offered by scientific grids. By presenting both the simulation and steering client as Grid services, it is then possible to make use of standard Grid infrastructure to manage communication and steering.

Some recent approaches to computational steering offer interactive simulation results by switching between a hierarchy of computational grids [54]. For fast response, the simulation computes on a low resolution grid, switching to higher resolutions when the user is inactive for a certain time frame. A further approach, is to keep the grid resolution constant, but adjust the degree of the polynomial used in p-FEM methods [55]. A lower p provides less accurate solutions but significantly faster.

4.2 EXTENDING STEERING APPROACHES WITH AN APPROXIMATION LAYER

The classical computational steering approaches presented so far rely on the almost immediate availability of simulation results. For some simulations this is possible when given a large availability of computing resources and a corresponding scalability of the application with an increasing number of computational nodes.

There are many situations where only limited computing resources are simultaneously available or the simulation code does not scale to deliver interactive output. To overcome such settings, a valuable idea is to move computational effort to a time previous to the actual use of computational steering techniques. Such offline computed data is then used to reduce computational effort in the productive phase of actual steering.

The approach proposed in this work is to place an approximation layer on top of the high-fidelity simulation. Acting as a preview to the simulation behavior, such a layer delivers approximate results, but in an interactive manner. Being the base for constructing the approximation, the simulation still remains the central part of the exploration process. It delivers results during the exploration, albeit only in the background.

The proposed method thus comes down to a trade off between accuracy and interactivity. The initial interactive solutions are delivered by the approximation layer, while the full simulation results are delivered with a certain delay. If the delay is significant, a scheduling of the full simulations is done, so that the results are available during the next exploration session.

The notion of *steering*, as in changing parameters and visualizing simulation outcome, is unchanged. With the approximation layer, not only does steering become interactive, but valuable knowledge can be extracted from the pre-computed data and presented during steering.

4.3 STEERING AND INSIGHT

While one goal of computational steering is insight in the underlying simulation, there are hardly any tools available to guide the steering process itself. The parameter space $\mathcal{P}$ given by a moderate number of parameters (2-10) can still be quite large even for an interactive exploration. Indicators of where to focus the exploration are valuable.

There have been some efforts to guide the search in the solution space. Matkovic et al. [60][59] employ a combination of automatic and interactive optimization workflow, where domain expert knowledge is used to interactively select data points (parameter combinations) and approximate values in a continuous region of the simulation space using regression. The "best" points in that continuous region, based on the specified constraints and objectives, are then suggested as next points to be considered for expert investigation. The accuracy of the regression model is improved with the newly added points.

Burrows et al. [11] investigated a bridge simulation with similar goals – efficiency and insight. They see the mining of simulation data as an approach to extract knowledge and decision rules from simulation results. The acquired knowledge is then used to provide preliminary answers and immediate feedback if an accurate analysis is not at hand or if waiting for the actual simulation results would considerably slow down the interaction between a human designer and the computer. The mapping from the design space to the solution space is learned by clustering aggregated snapshots. For new design parameters, the mapping returns similar designs (k-nearest neighbor). The clustering itself is also used to offer insight as to which parameter combinations lead to similar bridge designs.

Such methods aim to go beyond the efficient delivery of simulation results for given parameters. The next step is to "steer" the user to relevant parameter combinations, by offering information collected and aggregated in advance.

5

INTERACTIVE COMPUTATIONAL STEERING WITH SURROGATE MODELS

This chapter formulates the idea of surrogate-supported computational steering that satisfies two main exploration goals: interactivity and insight. First we identify the requirements a surrogate model must fulfill and afterwards continue with the presentation of the general surrogate model process. In line with the intrusive/non-intrusive distinction, sparse grids are motivated as non-intrusive surrogate models due to their favorable computational requirements and inherent extensible structure. On the intrusive branch, we present an extension to the POD-DEIM method, based on DEIM *locality* which reduces even more the cost of intrusive surrogate-based exploration.

5.1 REQUIREMENTS AND CHALLENGES

Interactivity

In classical steering the researcher usually faces a screen or a visualization system and actively changes simulation parameters. Based on the observed result, he then decides which next change to investigate. The responses of a system to the actions of the researcher serve as continuity of the exploration process. Thus, as a first requirement, a surrogate for a computational intensive simulation must deliver new data at interactive rates. Depending on the task at hand, different kinds of responses and response delays are psychologically acceptable. Take for example the two main types of exploration patterns common in visual computational steering. In a *parameter sweep*, the user continuously increments a single parameter, being interested in its influence on the behavior of the simulation. A response time of no more than 0.2 seconds was found to be suitable for such user continuous actions [64, 85]. The task of *parameter comparison* involves switching between two or more parameter combinations and afterwards judging the differences. For this task a response time of up to 2 seconds [64, 85] would still allow for an uninterrupted thought process. Both reaction times set a high bar for any simulation code, but also for surrogates.

Accuracy

What-if analyses or visual exploration aim to reveal main characteristics, rough trends, and in general provide an intuitive insight in the underlying simulation. Thus, as a second requirement, the *accuracy* of the data extracted from the surrogate must capture the defining simulation behavior, but need not necessarily deliver engineering precision. In general, the more accurate a surrogate model is the more computational intensive it becomes (either offline or online) and, as a result, less responsive.

Extensibility

Based on user input, the surrogate model should be extensible during the online phase (Fig. 12 extends Fig. 3). This allows the improvement of the accuracy in regions of relevance to the investigation. For simulations which are not interactive, but can deliver new snapshots during the online session, it must be possible for the surrogate to incorporate new results online without completely rebuilding the low-fidelity model.

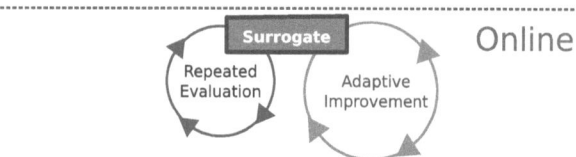

Figure 12: Not only is the surrogate evaluated in the online phase, but its accuracy can be improved at user request.

Indicators

One further selection criteria among the different methods is the availability or simplicity of deriving exploration indicators. The parameter space is usually large, but significant changes tend to be localized to certain smaller areas. For example, sensitivity analysis [84, 34] is a collection of methods which identify such areas. A surrogate should allow the cheap computation of such indicators or offer itself valuable exploration support.

A last challenge is to fulfill all the previous requirements in a comfortable framework. The construction of the surrogate for a new code should be unproblematic and the interface to the visualization components should allow a fast coupling and, as a result, a fast deployment.

5.2 NON-INTRUSIVE: SPARSE GRIDS AS SURROGATE MODELS

The interpolatory approach of sparse grids places them in the category of data fit reduced order models, i.e. an interpolant is fitted to a specific set of precomputed simulations and new solutions are extracted as linear combinations of the initial snapshots. This work proposes and evaluates sparse grids as surrogate models for supporting computational steering and argues that sparse grids fulfill the previous requirements for a great range of simulation functions. We briefly touch on each requirement.

Performance results in Chap. 6 show that the online phase is not costly and scales very well with the size of the snapshots. This fact is not easy to achieve with other surrogate models. Even more, the sparse grid surrogate model can be improved very efficiently even in the online phase. In contrast, other methods such as regression or Kriging require the repeated solution of large systems of equations and thus cannot be extended on-the-fly in the online phase.

Based on the classification of surrogate models in Chap. 2, sparse grid surrogates are non-intrusive models which treat the underlying simulation as a black box that delivers snapshots $\tilde{u}^\mu$ for the requested parameter combinations. If the simulation function is smooth within the chosen parameter ranges (see [10]), the accuracy of sparse grid interpolation is competitive with full grid interpolation. The smoothness of the focus applications presented in Chap. 1 is not a priori known, but with adaptive sparse grids we can relax the smoothness requirements and invest sampling points based on the local gradient information. The results achieved in Chap. 7 show that for all considered applications the obtained empirical accuracy is well suited for capturing the main features of each simulation.

The proposed surrogate model has a hierarchical structure which can be used for an incremental snapshot construction but also to indicate where change in the function response mostly happens. The size of the hierarchical increment together with the refinement concentration provide valuable indicators as to areas of change and thus importance in the parameter space.

5.2.1 Offline Phase

Typical to many surrogates, a number of high-fidelity simulations needs to be first performed and stored. The choice corresponds to a selection of parameter combinations from $\mathcal{P}_S$. For projection based methods or most data fit models, the most straightforward way is to use a random or uniform sampling. While easy to implement, there are also other methods grouped under the notion of Design of Experiments (DoE) (see [91] for the general idea) that aim to maximize the amount of information gained from a limited number of snapshots. Some examples are Latin Hypercube Sampling (LHS), Orthogonal Array Design (OAD) and Uniform Design (UD) (see [36] for an overview).

For the sparse grid surrogate model, the parameter domain $\mathcal{P}$ is sampled based on the sparse grid discretization by computing snapshots $\mathbf{u}(\mu_1), \ldots, \mathbf{u}(\mu_M) \in \mathbb{R}^N$ where the parameters $\mu_1, \ldots, \mu_M \in \mathcal{P}$ are the coordinate axes of the sparse grid interpolation points (see Fig. 13). The number of pre-computed snapshots is thus equal to the number of discretization points in the sparse grid. As all computation happens offline, we can afford to compute reasonably many snapshots. Of course there are computational, time, or even processing constraints that can limit the size of the actual sampling (and thus sparse grid). The required sampling size depends on the smoothness of the simulation function and the accuracy the surrogate should offer.

The surrogate is a map $\tilde{\mathbf{u}} : \mathcal{P} \to \mathbb{R}^N$ that approximates the full simulation $\mathbf{u}$. $\tilde{\mathbf{u}}$ can be seen as a vector-valued sparse grid function (or, alternatively, a vector of sparse grids), where each component function $\tilde{\mathbf{u}}^1, \ldots, \tilde{\mathbf{u}}^N : \mathcal{P} \to \mathbb{R}$ can be represented as a linear combination

$$\tilde{\mathbf{u}}^i(\mu) = \sum_{j=1}^{M} \alpha_j^i \phi_j(\mu), \qquad (33)$$

where $\phi_1, \ldots, \phi_M$ are the hierarchical basis functions and the coefficients $\alpha_1^i, \ldots, \alpha_M^i$ are the hierarchical coefficients or surpluses corresponding to the i-th component function $\tilde{\mathbf{u}}^i$. Let $\mathbf{u}^i(\mu)$ be the i-th discretization node of the snapshot $\mathbf{u}(\mu)$ with parameter μ. The i-th component function $\tilde{\mathbf{u}}^i$ of $\tilde{\mathbf{u}}$ is the interpolant of the pairs

$$\left\{ (\mu_1, \mathbf{u}^i(\mu_1)), \ldots, (\mu_M, \mathbf{u}^i(\mu_M)) \right\}, \qquad (34)$$

where the parameters $\mu_1, \ldots, \mu_M$ are the sampling points and the values at the i-th node of the corresponding snapshots are the function values. This component-wise view illustrates how a single node in the snapshot is interpolated. However, in the following we are interested in extracting all nodes within a snapshot and talk about $\tilde{\mathbf{u}}$ as block and not component-wise.

The next step is to perform a basis transformation on each snapshot in $\mathcal{P}_s$. Called *hierarchization*, this transformation step is specific to the sparse grid surrogate model and also concludes the offline phase.

5.2 NON-INTRUSIVE: SPARSE GRIDS AS SURROGATE MODELS

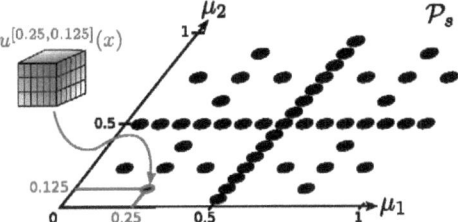

Figure 13: Sparse grid sampling $\mathcal{P}_s$ in a two-dimensional parameter space. The point coordinates denote the (normalized) parameter combinations, for which simulations need to be performed and stored.

Let $\mathcal{H}^{\mu_j} \subseteq \mathcal{P}_s$ be the set of hierarchical ancestors of sampling point μ_j (see Chap. 3),

$$\mathcal{H}^{\mu_j} = \{\, \mu_k \mid \mu_k \text{ is hier. ancestor of } \mu_j \,\}. \tag{35}$$

Hierarchization denotes the transformation of all sample snapshots u^{μ_j}, $\mu_j \in \mathcal{P}_s$ into their representation as hierarchical increments $\alpha_j = \alpha^{\mu_j}$, i.e the surpluses. Hierarchization is a necessary step before the model $\tilde{u}(x, \mu)$ can be evaluated. The surplus block α_j depends on the surpluses of all hierarchical ancestors μ_k in $\mathcal{H}^{\mu_j}$ as

$$\alpha_j := u_j^\mu - \tilde{u}_j^\mu, \tag{36}$$

$$\alpha_j := u_j^\mu - \underbrace{\sum_{\mu_k \in \mathcal{H}^{\mu_j}} \alpha_k \cdot \varphi_k(\mu_j)}_{\text{interpolant without } \mu_j}, \tag{37}$$

which motivates the name surplus: the difference needed to correct the current sparse grid interpolant so that it interpolates additive at μ_j.

5.2.2 Online Phase

The online phase starts once all snapshots are hierarchized. At this point, $\tilde{u}$ can be evaluated over the parameter space $\mathcal{P}$, using information from the set of sampling points $\mathcal{P}_s$. The evaluation at point $\mu \in \mathcal{P}$ is obtained as a linear combination of the M weighted basis functions corresponding to the M grid points,

$$\tilde{u}(x, \mu) := \sum_{j=1}^{M} \alpha_j(x) \cdot \phi_j(\mu). \tag{38}$$

The assembly of the summation terms involves three central aspects.

Identification of the affected basis functions

Sparse grid basis functions ϕ_j on the same level have disjunct support but overlap with basis on different levels. It can be easily seen how the support size varies in the illustrations of Fig. 7. Thus, only a subset of basis functions will be affected by a certain evaluation, fact that is speculated to increase the computational efficiency of the evaluation (not all bases are involved). Evaluating the surrogate model at point μ therefore requires first to identify the set $\mathcal{A}^\mu$ of affected basis functions with respect to evaluation point μ,

$$\mathcal{A}^\mu := \{\phi_j \mid j = 1, \ldots, M \wedge \phi_j(\mu) \neq 0\}. \tag{39}$$

For a two-dimensional regular sparse grid of level three, Fig. 14 shows which snapshots (smaller cubes) need to be collected in order to interpolate a new snapshot at the evaluation point marked with a triangle. Note that working with the full set of basis functions (or grid points, respectively) instead of $\mathcal{A}^\mu$ is not an option as typically $M \gg |\mathcal{A}^\mu|$ which would result in significantly more effort in the next step.

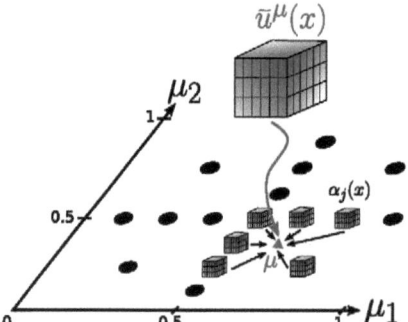

Figure 14: An example for a sparse grid interpolation: for the (triangle marked) parameter combination μ, the value $\tilde{u}^\mu(x)$ of the approximated snapshot is constructed as a sum of the weighted hierarchical coefficients $\alpha_j(x)$, marked with cubes.

Combination of the weighted surpluses:

From a mathematical point of view there is little to discuss about the sum (38). Even though simple to express, efficient gather and reduce strategies need to be considered for its algorithmic implementation. It is the critical operation of the online phase, and its performance is crucial to a smooth user experience, as detailed in Chap. 6. This step can and should be completely separated from the first step of identifying the data dependencies.

Improvement of the model

Last but not least, the set $\mathcal{P}_s$ of sampling points can be improved. A user steered what-if analysis demands an extensible approach. This means allowing for an incremental improvement of the approximation quality during the online phase in regions where the user sees fit.

If the initial sampling of the parameter space does not capture well the features of the underlying simulation function **u**, automatic or user driven refinement of points from $\mathcal{P}_s$ is employed. The acquisition and integration of the new simulation snapshots relies on steps from the offline phase. The reduction operation *hierarchization* needs to be performed for each new simulation result $\mathbf{u}_j^\mu$ by applying (37). As this boils down to the cost of an evaluation plus a block subtraction, it does not interfere with the user experience, an important requirement for on-the-fly extension.

5.2.3 Visual Analytics for Steering

So far, with the sparse grid surrogate approximated solutions can be interactively delivered to the exploring engineer. The question which now rises is whether we can speed up the exploration by highlighting (in some sense) *relevant* areas in the parameter domain. Such areas would indicate parameters or parameter ranges to which the simulation is most sensible and thus visually guide the explorer to steer the surrogate to those parameter combinations and inspect the approximated simulation snapshot. In this sense, the surrogate contributes itself to the what-if analysis.

By applying the surrogate models based on sparse grid interpolation described so far, we obtain a function which has a hierarchical structure given as a linear combination of hierarchical basis functions with hierarchical coefficients. A hierarchical coefficient corresponding to a grid point (or basis function) is a crucial piece of information as it indicates how important that grid point is for the function: A small absolute value can only lead to a small change in the function, whereas a large value means that the basis function significantly influences the function. A through discussion of these properties of the hierarchical basis can be found in e.g. [75, 10].

As mentioned, the sparse grid can be constructed in an adaptive manner. The adaptivity is based on the hierarchical coefficients which reflect local smoothness. Hence, the refinement in the parameter space contains valuable information about the influence of parameters and is an indicator of parameter sensitivity.

Both indicators – hierarchical coefficients and refinement – are used with visual analytics tools. First, we employ scatter plot matrices to visualize the multi-dimensional sparse grid (see Fig. 15, [17]). A scatter plot matrix is a scheme of scatter plots where each column contains the same X axis and each row the same Y axis. For a sparse grid each subplot is a projection of all high-dimensional grid points onto two dimensions. Thus, due to the refinement criterion, the number and location of the projected points indicates where, with respect to the projected parameters, changes happen. We furthermore enhance the scatter plot by drawing the grid points as circles whose radius correspond to the hierarchical coefficient. This shows the relative importance of each point and the magnitude of change.

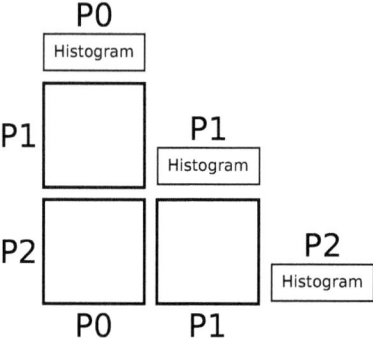

Figure 15: Scatter plot matrix with histograms for three parameters.

Another visual analytics tool we consider, is a weighted parallel coordinates plot (sketched in Fig. 16, introduced in [45] with applicability examples in [53]). To plot a set of d-dimensional points, d axes are drawn vertically and equally spaced. A point is represented as a polyline with vertices on the parallel axes; the position of the vertex on the i-th axis corresponds to the i-th coordinate of the point. In our case, the axes are given by the parameters of the simulation. Each sparse grid point can then be represented by a polyline connecting each axis (dimension) at the value of the corresponding parameter. We further extend this plot by weighting and color-coding each polyline with the absolute value of the hierarchical coefficient.

5.3 MODEL IMPROVEMENT THROUGH ADAPTIVE REFINEMENT

Any surrogate model is an approximation to the high-fidelity model. The type of used surrogate, the type of the underlying simulation function $\mathbf{u}^\mu$, or the initial sampling $\mathcal{P}_s$ all influence the degrees of accuracy of the delivered snapshots $\tilde{\mathbf{u}}^\mu$.

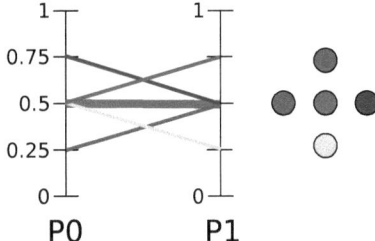

Figure 16: Weighed parallel coordinates. Each vertical line represents one dimension (two in this case). Each line corresponds to a point in the sparse grid discretization, formed by connecting the vertical axes at the corresponding coordinate values. The thickness of each line corresponds to the hierarchical coefficient at that point.

For sufficiently smooth functions, sparse grids reduce the number of grid points by orders of magnitude to only $\mathcal{O}(M \log(M)^{d-1})$, while keeping a similar accuracy as in the full grid case [10]. For computational steering the nature of the underlying simulation function is usually not known and theoretical error boundaries are not available. Even in such a case the accuracy of the interpolant $\tilde{u}$ can be improved by choosing a more appropriate set of sampling points $\mathcal{P}_s$.

Either during construction or in the online phase, spatial (local) adaptivity is used to construct a more accurate interpolant. The adaptivity described in Chap. 3 chooses points with the highest hierarchical coefficients and adds their children to the current grid. For the surrogate model this translates in the selection of certain parameters combinations μ_i which are added to the sampling set. Refinement thus improves the current model by an appropriate small choice of points which helps keep the cost of the offline phase down.

As a starting point, a coarse sparse grid (as in Fig. 13) is used and, based on a suitable adaptivity criterion, points are added in those regions of the domain with most change (criteria based). The surrogate setup consists of a succession of refinement steps.

5.3.1 *Refinement Procedure*

Given a fixed budget of M offline snapshots to be used for the surrogate, a refinement step proceeds as follows. First, candidates for refinement are identified. These are all sparse grid points on the last level. Not all candidate points need to be refined at once as a refinement step introduces new points, which under the considered criteria might be more suitable for further refinement than some of the current candidates. Typically ≈ 10 points with the highest refinement indicators are selected and all 2^d children are added to the sparse grid. Snapshots for all new points need to be then computed in an automated process. After the results are available, the current repository is consolidated by mapping each new snapshot to its hierarchical representation (see Eq. 37) and adding it to the repository storage. Sketched, the refinement process involves the following steps:

```
while repository size < M

  identifyRefinablePoints()

  for each refinable point
    computeRefinementIndicator()
  end for

  sortRefinablePointsByIndicator()
  refineFirstFewPoints()
  performSimulations()
  consolidateRepository()

end while
```

5.3.2 *Refinement Criteria*

We have seen how the refinement process is implemented, but there is still the open question as to which refinement criterion to use. In the case where the sparse grid interpolates a single (possibly aggregated) scalar value, a simple – though typically very effective – criterion for adaptive refinement is to select the refinement candidates with the highest absolute values of their hierarchical coefficients α_i.

However, in a computational steering scenario the refinement candidates are *blocks of hierarchical coefficients*. Each entry in this block corresponds to a node in the discretization grid of the simulation. Furthermore, for applications with multiple Degree of Freedom (DoF) per discretization node, an entry in the hierarchical block also corresponds to a particular DoF. Figure 17 illustrates this case with a reactive flow simulation which will be considered in detail in Chap. 7.

With multiple values per sparse grid point, the refinement still involves hierarchical increments. Only now there is more choice as to which part of the block of increments to use for the refinement. This choice can be thought of as an *objective*. One such objective would be to construct a surrogate that, on average, approximates equally well the full snapshot. This implies a good interpolation on average for all

5.3 MODEL IMPROVEMENT THROUGH ADAPTIVE REFINEMENT

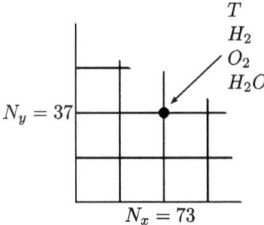

Figure 17: The simulation domain is discretized with $N = N_x \times N_y = 73 \times 37$ nodes. At each node the temperature T and concentrations of three reaction species are stored: hydrogen H_2, oxygen O_2, and water H_2O.

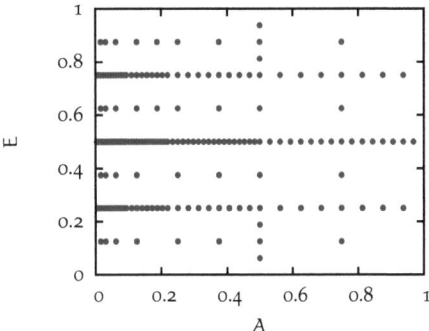

Figure 18: Refinement pattern for a budget of $M \approx 200$ and using criterium (40).

DoFs at all N discretization nodes. The refinement indicator for block α_i is then defined as:

$$I_1(\alpha_i) = \frac{1}{p}\sum_{k=1}^{p} \frac{1}{N} \sum_{j=1}^{N} (\alpha_i(k,j))^2 \tag{40}$$

where p is the number of DoFs. The refinement criterion selects the points with the largest indicators for refinement. Figure 18 shows the refinement pattern using indicator I_1 with a budget of $\approx$200 snapshots. A scaling of the DoFs should be considered if the ranges are significantly different.

A second objective focuses on a specific degree of freedom at a specific location in the discretized domain. For example, the temperature T at coordinates [0, 0] should be approximated best with the purpose

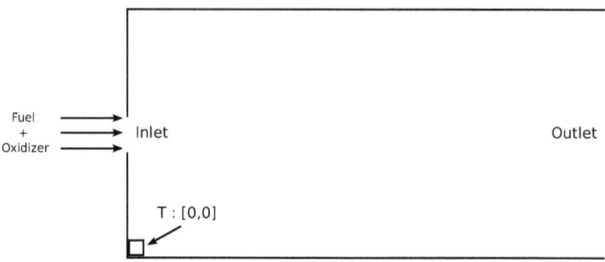

Figure 19: Only the temperature T at node [0,0] is used as refinement indicator.

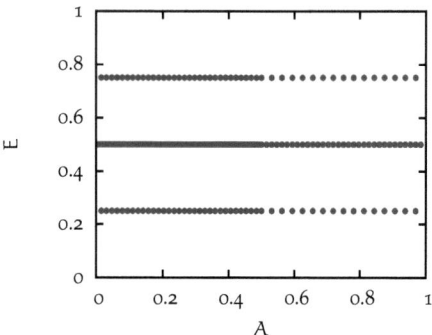

Figure 20: Refinement pattern for a budget of M ≈ 200 and using indicator (41) for T at [0,0]. Notice that refinement is necessary only in A to best capture the temperature at this point.

of comparing it to experimental measurements at the same point. We are still interested in visually depicting the full solution, but the temperature at that particular point should be best interpolated with the budget of M points. The refinement indicator for block i for this objective is:

$$I_2(\alpha_i) = \sum_{j=a}^{b} (\alpha_i(k,j))^2 \qquad (41)$$

where a, b are lower and upper limits of the subset of nodes under consideration and k is the selected DoF. Refinement outcomes for using I_2 are presented in Fig. 20 and 22 with the setup described in Fig. 19 and 21 respectively.

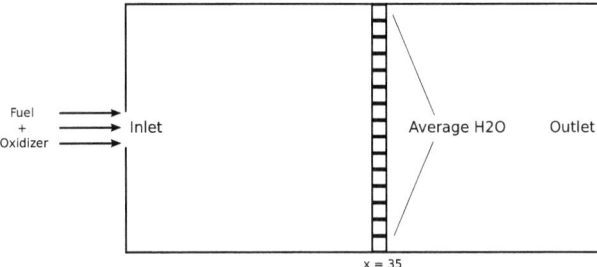

Figure 21: The H_2O concentration along the line $x = 35$ is considered for computing the refinement criteria.

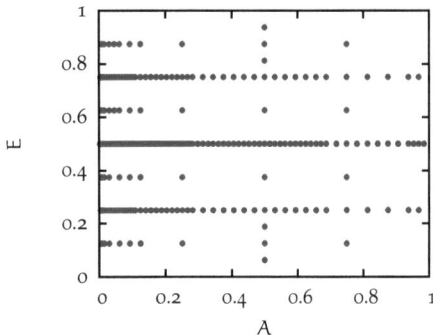

Figure 22: Refinement pattern for a budget of $M = 200$ and using indicator (41) for H_2O along $x = 35$. The refinement pattern follows the one for indicator (40) with small changes. The H_2O concentration for DoFs with $x = 35$ has a similar sensitivity to the parameters.

5.4 STEERING WITH INTRUSIVE SURROGATE MODELS

Intrusive surrogate models such as Proper Orthogonal Decomposition combined with the Discrete Empirical Interpolation Method (POD-DEIM) solve the original partial differential equation (PDE) but in a reduced space (revisit Chap. 2). The similarity with the original simulation enables this method to deliver snapshots which tend to be more accurate than their non-intrusive counter-parts. Also time dependent simulations are captured more naturally with the POD-DEIM method as time maintains the same nature as in the high-fidelity model and is not considered just an additional parameter. We next describe the offline/online usage pattern present also with intrusive surrogate models and an extension to the POD-DEIM with steering implications.

5.4.1 Offline Phase

POD-DEIM requires two sets of orthogonal projection bases $V \in \mathbb{R}^{n_{POD} \times N}$ and $U \in \mathbb{R}^{n_{DEIM} \times N}$. n_{POD} and n_{DEIM} are the chosen number of global and respectively non-linear POD modes. V is computed from the SVD of a set of snapshots $x^{\mu_1}, \ldots, x^{\mu_M} \in \mathbb{R}^N$ while U from the SVD of the corresponding non-linear snapshots $f(x^{\mu_1}), \ldots, f(x^{\mu_M}) \in \mathbb{R}^N$. Unlike the sparse grid surrogate, the sampling $\mathcal{P}_s$ of the parameter domain $\mathcal{P}$ has no restrictions and can be constructed either uniformly, randomly, or with DoE.

With V available, initial state vectors and system matrices are reduced:

$$x_r^0 = V^T x^0 \qquad (42)$$
$$A_r = V^T A V \qquad (43)$$

The DEIM basis and the extraction matrix P are then used to compute the nonlinear approximation term which will be used during the online phase:

$$V^T U (P^T U)^{-1} \qquad (44)$$

5.4.2 Online Phase

For POD-DEIM the online phase distinguishes itself very little from the solution of the original PDE. Instead of the initial system of equations, the PDE has now the form:

$$\dot{x}_r(t) = A_r x_r(t) + V^T U (P^T U)^{-1} F(P^T x(t)) \qquad (45)$$
$$x_r^0 = x_r(0) \qquad (46)$$

The accuracy up of the POD-DEIM method can be controlled by choosing the number of global POD modes m_{POD} and the number of DEIM points n_{DEIM}. These two adjustments can be used in the steering process to obtain interactive response rates by choosing m_{POD} and n_{DEIM} so that for a problem of size $\mathcal{N}$ the solution is obtained close to real-time and the accuracy is satisfiable.

5.4.3 Improvement Through DEIM Locality

Due to real-time requirements we would like to lower n_{DEIM} (the number of evaluations of the nonlinear term) but at the same time we would like the accuracy of the interpolation to stay roughly unchanged. To tackle this, we note that the quality of the DEIM interpolation depends on the number and choice of DEIM points. While the number is fixed, there is still the flexibility to define their location.

Before describing an improvement in this direction let us first illustrate the problem. The *"two peak"* function pictured in Fig. 23 (top) is an extension of Fig. 4 which adds a second non-linear singularity in the opposite corner. By applying DEIM on this function we notice that the DEIM points are almost equally spread between the two peaks (see Fig. 23, bottom). This is exactly the expected behavior and shows that the method can successfully identify important (high variance) points. However, the accuracy of the method decreases as there are not sufficiently many DEIM points in the fixed budget to approximate both singularities with the same quality.

A solution is to construct *local* DEIM bases and corresponding DEIM points that are better suited to the underlying simulation behavior. At runtime the appropriate basis is selected and used. Such bases can be constructed by splitting either the parameter domain or the state space in several regions. In this work the former is presented while the dissertation of Benjamin Peherstorfer will detail the later. Ideas to adapt the reduced model to local characteristics have been also proposed for the reduced basis method [23, 24, 25, 41], POD based reduction [96, 86], empirical interpolation method [22], and also for DEIM [3].

The cost of the local DEIM approach changes as follows. In the offline phase, several runs of the original DEIM algorithm are needed but of smaller size, thus an increase in offline cost is to be expected. We are not bothered by this as for repeated evaluations of the surrogate, the offline phase DEIM costs are compensated. The positive aspect is that the computational costs of the online phase remain unchanged while the accuracy is significantly improved when compared to the original DEIM.

We now face the main question of how to construct "good" DEIM bases. For that, we need a *strategy* for splitting the parameter domain and a *criterion* which decides the quality of the splitting.

As a strategy, approaches such as recursive partitioning have been tried in other contexts [25] but become problematic for parameter domains of higher dimensionality (> 2). We therefore propose the use of *clustering* methods. Clustering is the grouping of a set of objects in

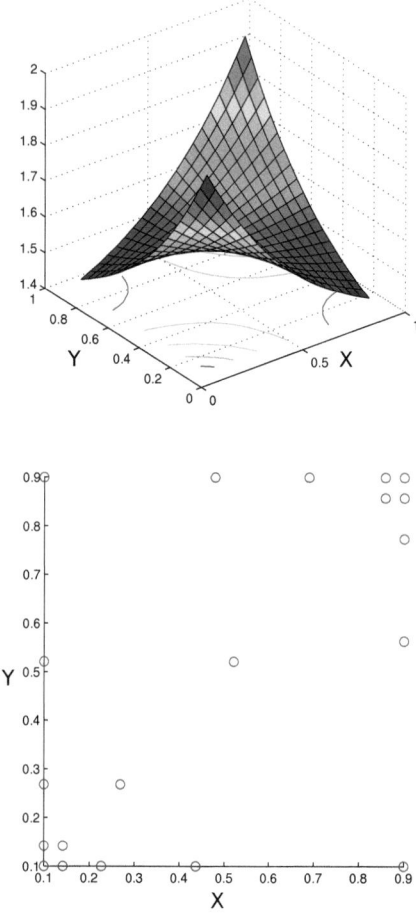

Figure 23: Two peak function (top) and corresponding DEIM points (bottom).

such a way that objects in the same cluster (DEIM basis) are more similar (criteria-based) to each other than to those in other clusters.

Algorithm 2 DEIM Residual-based Clustering

Input: X snapshots, k cluster count, U_i DEIM bases, P_i DEIM points
Output: clustering , cluster repartition for each snapshot X_j
  currentMinimumError ← inf
  for j = 1 to size(X) **do**
    for i = 1 to k **do**
      ϵ ← DEIMresidual(X_j, U_i, P_i)
      if ϵ < currentMinimumError **then**
        clustering[j] ← i
        currentMinimumError ← ϵ
      end if
    end for
  end for

The method proceeds by associating each snapshot with an initial cluster. The snapshots in each initial cluster are then used to compute initial U_i DEIM bases and corresponding P_i DEIM points. The clustering algorithm (sketched in Alg. 2) takes this initial configuration an outputs a new assignment of snapshots to clusters. This is done by checking each snapshot against each $\{U_i, P_i\}$ and allocating it to that cluster for which the criterion is minimum. As a criterion we use the DEIM residual

$$\text{DEIMresidual}(X_j, U_i, P_i) = \|X_j - U_i(P_i^T U_i)^{-1}(P_i^T X_j)\|_2 \quad (47)$$

which measures how well the snapshot X_j is interpolated by the basis U_i with DEIM points P_i. A related idea to cluster based on projection error was presented in [21].

The clustering algorithm is repeated until the clustering does not change or a maximum number of iterations have been performed. The last clustering is used to construct the bases and DEIM points used in the actual solving of the reduced PDE. To avoid large discontinuities at cluster borders, each cluster is enriched with a percentage of the neighboring clusters. This procedure is detailed in Appendix B.

Figure 24 depicts the clustering of the two-peak function with k = 4. It identifies very well the two singularities and groups points which share similar values in the same cluster. Next, let us verify if the clustering does indeed lead to better accuracy with the same number of points. Figure 25 confirms that with an increasing number of clusters the error decreases significantly for the two-peak problem.

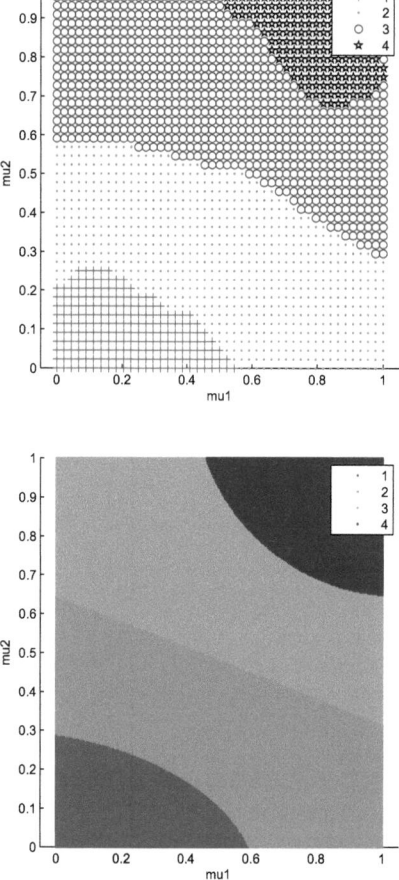

Figure 24: Top: k = 4 clustering for the two peak function. Bottom: corresponding classification.

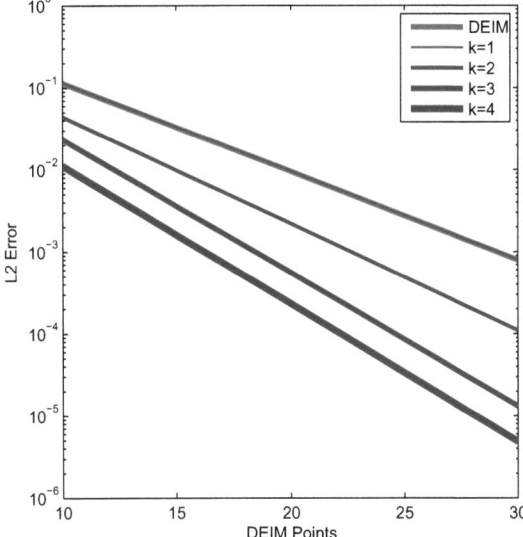

Figure 25: DEIM Accuracy for increasing cluster count (line thickness). A bit more that two digits of accuracy can be gained by using local DEIM bases.

To summarize, the intrusive POD-DEIM reduces the cost of solving reduced PDEs with computationally expensive non-linear terms by interpolating the non-linearity. If the problem exhibits localized non-linearities, the accuracy of the method can be further improved by isolating such non-linearities and constructing different bases for different areas in the parameter domain. For the two-peak function the results are very promising. In Chap. 7 we apply the intrusive approach to the reactive flow and also show improvements for this problem. While an improved accuracy is desirable, for our steering endeavor such improvements ultimately aim for a faster execution time (less n_{DEIM} points) for the same accuracy. We will elaborate on this point of view in Chap. 7.

5.5 SUMMARY

In this chapter, we have presented the idea of computational steering augmented by surrogate models. The surrogate model runs either alone or on top of a high-fidelity simulation and delivers approximate but interactive results to a visualization system.

The choice of surrogate model has been motivated by a set of criteria required by interactive computational steering. First, the low-fidelity model must capture the global behavior of the high-fidelity model. Second, any evaluation must deliver results in less than 0.2 seconds. Third, it must be extensible on-the-fly during its usage. Fourth, for what-if analyses, is should offer or allow the computation of parameter sensibility information.

We have developed a non-intrusive surrogate model based on sparse grid interpolation. The sparse grid is placed in the parameter space where each point corresponds to a high-fidelity snapshot. In order to extract new results, multi-dimensional piecewise linear interpolation is performed among precomputed snapshots. The sparse grid surrogate fulfills the previous criteria. It offers cheap evaluation consisting of a weighed summation of data blocks and is extensible by adaptive refinement. Its accuracy and sensibility information will be the topics of Chap. 7.

With LDEIM we have introduced an extension to the classical DEIM that reduces the number of DEIM points needed to approximate a non-linear function. By clustering snapshots we have constructed a series of local DEIM bases that better capture areas of similar behavior. Due to the similarity within clusters, fewer DEIM points are needed to approximate the non-linear PDE term. This leads to an decrease in response time for the intrusive surrogate model.

6

SYSTEM DESIGN

The evaluation of the sparse grid surrogate model consists of a linear combination of blocks of hierarchical coefficients. While this is indeed a mathematically simple operation, the data structure used by the sparse grid and the number and size of individual blocks directly influence how efficiently it can actually be computed. In order to achieve close to interactive rates for reasonably sized problems, we take advantage of modern hardware. In this chapter, we propose and describe in detail several data organization concepts and parallelization approaches for the evaluation operation.

The result of the simulation can be of different types (scalar, scalar field, vector field) and requires different visualization techniques, such as color mapping for scalar fields or streamlines for vector fields. We present a small and flexible interface to several visualization tools, where the sparse grid surrogate is implemented as a black box data repository which delivers approximated snapshot data for any parameter combination within the $\mathcal{P}$ domain. The repository sees only the data and is transparent to mesh information or number of degrees of freedom. While the efficiency of the evaluation is critical, also loading the result in the buffer of any visualization tool leads to performance penalty. This is particularly important when a distributed repository is driving a distributed multi-display visualization system, as we will describe in this chapter.

Computational steering with surrogate models is a continuous, but incremental exploration process, where the current surrogate model is gradually improved by refining certain sparse grid points based on the hierarchical increments α_i. This triggers the computation of new simulation snapshots which are integrated in the current model in order to improve the accuracy. The implementation of this workflow is also treated in this chapter.

6.1 SYSTEM ARCHITECTURE FOR EFFICIENT DATA DELIVERY

The implementation of our surrogate should result in a system which is easily connected to a visualization environment and delivers results at interactive rates. To achieve this, an integrated system is proposed that manages offline snapshot computation, surrogate construction, and evaluation during online visualization.

```
            Repository Type
    ┌────┬──────┬──────────────────┐
    │GPU │ CPU  │  Distributed CPU │
    └────┴──────┴──────────────────┘
    ────┼──────┼─────────────────────▶
        6      24
       Available Main Memory (GB)
```

Figure 26: The memory requirement of the surrogate model is given by the size of the high-fidelity snapshot multiplied with the number of points in the sparse grid. Based on this number the appropriate implementation is to be used.

For offline snapshot computation, the high-fidelity model needs to be automatically triggered, in order to pre-compute snapshots for the parameter combinations in $\mathcal{P}_s$. The approach followed here is to use a custom Python wrapper for the considered simulation code. The wrapper reads the parameter values, triggers the run, and places the result at a designated location. The same mechanism is used online, when a refinement is triggered.

The surrogate is constructed by converting the snapshots to hierarchical increments. This step can occur in the offline phase, and within the implementation presented in this chapter, also at program startup. We note, that for regular sparse grids the hierarchization operation has been efficiently parallelized (see [12, 68]) so that both initialization and extension can be also moved in the online phase.

To organize data access during the online phase, all snapshots are loaded into a *data repository* which is responsible for data loading, query and extension of the surrogate model. For sparse grid interpolation all snapshots are considered a vector of nodes which correspond to a structured or unstructured mesh. In the simplest implementation the snapshots are stored as a contiguous memory block in traversal-order. Each block is indexed by a unique identifier which is then used to lookup blocks during evaluation. The repository is also in control of the simulation wrapper and can trigger new runs, either in the offline or online phase.

With multi-core CPUs, graphics processing units (GPUs), hybrid CPU-GPU, or compute clusters, modern architectures offer an interesting set of parallelization possibilities each with certain advantages as well as implementation challenges. The data repository, together with the surrogate concept, is targeted at small (multi-core CPU) to mid-sized systems (small enterprise clusters). Thus, we focus next on implementation strategies for the sparse grid repository on such systems.

The choice of the repository implementation is given by the storage requirements of the surrogate model. For efficiency reasons, blocks of hierarchical coefficients are always loaded into main memory. The implementation to be used (see Fig. 26) is decided by the capacity of the repository to store all snapshots. Next, we elaborate repository implementations for GPU, CPU, and distributed-CPU versions.

6.1.1 *GPU Repository*

The first implementation of an efficient repository involves moving the data and most of the computation to the GPU. It is separated into a CPU and a GPU component, where the CPU component implements the logic of the surrogate model while the GPU component is responsible for data storage as well as fast data delivery when the model is evaluated. We refer to the components as *host* and *device*, a common terminology in GPU computing [72].

Both the hierarchization (37) and the evaluation (38) can be expressed in terms of Single-precision real Alpha X Plus Y (SAXPY) operations. SAXPY (see [38]) is a Level 1 (vector) operation in the Basic Linear Algebra Subprograms (BLAS) package, common among vector processors. SAXPY is a combination of scalar multiplication and vector addition in the form:

$$Y \leftarrow AX + Y \qquad (48)$$

where A is a scalar, and X and Y are vectors. Exemplified on the evaluation, Y is the accumulated result $\tilde{u}$, A is the value of an affected basis function at the evaluation point $\phi(\mu)$ and X is the corresponding block of hierarchical coefficients α_i. The GPU repository uses CUDA's SIMT (Single Instruction Multiple Thread) parallelism ([56, 70] to perform the series of SAXPY operations (see [6]).

CPU component (host)

The host acts as the frontend of the repository towards the application side. It creates and manages the adaptive sparse grid, a data structure based on hash maps [75]. Each entry in the hash map stores a unique identifier to a block of hierarchical coefficients. The number of points in the grid is moderate (usually less than 1000), which makes the managing data structure small, while the referenced data is very large. It thus makes sense to keep the grid management on the CPU and invest parallelization effort in the operations that work on the blocks. Therefore, the host maintains the complex structure of the sparse grid surrogate model and delegates tasks to the device, its dedicated worker.

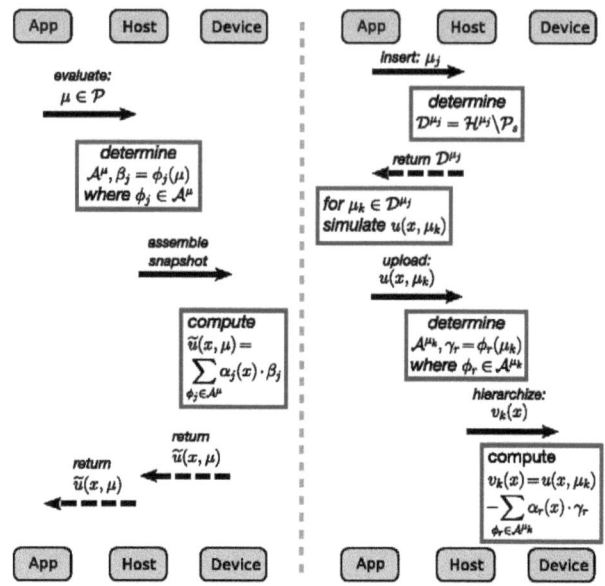

Figure 27: Sequence diagrams for the evaluation of the surrogate model at point $\mu \in \mathcal{P}$ (left), and the extension of the model by a new snapshot $\mathbf{u}(x, \mu_j)$, where μ_j is a valid sparse grid sampling point with $\mu_j \notin \mathcal{P}_s$ (right).

GPU component (device)

The device is the backend of the repository, responsible for data and compute intensive tasks. No knowledge about the surrogate model is necessary to perform the hierarchization and evaluation tasks given by the host, which are always related to (37) and (38).

In these equations very long vectors (the snapshots $\mathbf{u}^{\mu_i}$ and surpluses α_i) are added or subtracted, making this task memory-bound. This is a suitable task for a processor with high memory bandwidth like a GPU. Our test system uses Nvidia's Tesla C2070 and Intel's Westmere processors (dual hexa-core Xeon X5690, 3.46GHz). The Tesla C2070 offers a specified bandwidth of 144GB/s. It is therefore a good choice for the backend in charge of these operations. In comparison, the theoretical bandwidth of Intel's Westmere processor is specified as 32GB/s. However only around 21GB/s can actually be achieved (measured with STREAM benchmark [62, 61]).

In the following, the interplay of device, host, and application is discussed for the two scenarios in which the repository is accessed (also follow Fig. 27):

1. Evaluation at position $\mu \in \mathcal{P}$: The host determines the set of affected basis functions $\mathcal{A}^\mu$, evaluates them and passes the resulting values $\beta_j := \phi_j(\mu), \phi_j \in \mathcal{A}^\mu$ to the device. The interpolated snapshot $\tilde{\mathbf{u}}^\mu$ is computed on the GPU using SAXPY operations.

2. Extension by the inclusion of a new snapshot $\mathbf{u}^{\mu_j}$: $\mathcal{P}_s$ is extended with the valid new sparse grid sampling point $\mathbf{u}^{\mu_j}$. The host first determines all unfulfilled hierarchical dependencies $\mathcal{D}^{\mu_j} = \mathcal{H}^{\mu_j} \setminus \mathcal{P}_s$, i.e., the hierarchical ancestors of μ_j missing from $\mathcal{P}_s$ which are required to ensure a valid grid structure. Once the high-fidelity snapshots for the $\mu_k \in \mathcal{D}^{\mu_j}$ are available, the host prepares the hierarchization of the new snapshots $\mathbf{u}^{\mu_k}$ by computing the respective weights $\gamma_r = \phi_r(\mu_k)$. With the γ_r, the device can efficiently perform hierarchization (37) and integrate the surpluses α_k into the model.

6.1.2 CPU-Only Repository

The evaluation operation, as a weighted sum of large blocks, is a memory-bound task. In our interactive setting, we want to apply the memory-bound summation also to large snapshots, hence our target platform should provide (1) a significant amount of memory (tens of GBs) and (2) high memory bandwidth. With up to 200 GB/s, GPUs may offer memory bandwidth several times higher than the 50–100 GB/s obtained on a state-of-the-art x86 CPU-based system. However, GPUs can only accommodate a small number of large snapshots due to the memory limit of $\leqslant$ 6 GB on current GPU architectures. The GPU repository thus copes very well with the second requirement, but is limited with respect to (1).

Non-Uniform Memory Access (NUMA) is a computer memory design characterized by faster memory access to memory units that are closer to the processors. Under NUMA, the processor can access its own local memory faster than non-local memory (memory local to another processor or memory shared between processors). As a result, with NUMA systems memory bandwidth scales with the number of NUMA cores, a feature which helps memory bound algorithms like the surrogate evaluation. To make use of this property on a NUMA system, the sparse grid operations must be translated in a multi-threaded implementation which is aware of the NUMA memory layout.

The NUMA-aware CPU repository implementation splits the evaluation work equally on the available cores. The repository is split snapshot-wise, where each part is loaded on the physical memory bank corresponding to a particular core. A first touch policy decides the affinity (binding) of the thread with respect to a core. For example, the first memory access for performing $\tilde{u}_\mu(x_0) = \tilde{u}_\mu(x_0) + \alpha_1 \phi_1(x_0)$ pins the thread 0 to the core associated with that memory bank. Subsequent operations will only work with repository data available in the local memory bank. This ensures high memory bandwidth which scales with the number of cores. Further optimizations include vectorization and cache optimizations. The speedup and response time obtained on our test NUMA architecture are discussed in Chap. 7.

6.1.3 *Distributed Snapshots for Large Repositories*

Both GPU and CPU-only repositories deliver fast results to the visualization as long as all hierarchized snapshots can be fitted in the GPU or main memory respectively. For example, a current high-end GPU featuring 6 GB of memory can store and combine up to 200 snapshots of size 3×128^3 floats. A system with 24 GB of main memory can store up to 800 snapshots of the same size. Depending on the dimensionality d of the parameter space, this might not be enough to ensure a good approximation quality. To mitigate this limitation, we use the combined memory of all available GPUs/CPUs to distribute the repository and thus store more snapshots. On each node n we construct the surrogate $\tilde{u}^\mu([x_{is} : x_{(i+1)s}]), i = 0 \ldots N-1$, for a slice of size s of the entire domain Ω. The GPU-distributed repository will thus use all available GPUs in the computing cluster to distribute snapshot slices. The CPU-distributed repository will use all available cluster main memory to do the same. Such a distribution allows for a flexible and load balanced computation of the final snapshot, but requires a gather operation in order to assemble the full snapshot for visualization.

A further enhancement could be to combine the GPU and CPU computing resources in a two phase evaluation. The grid points on the lower levels ($l = 1, 2, 3..$) are always involved in the evaluation. The SAXPY operations for those levels takes place on the GPU, while in a second phase, the CPU delivers the rest of the linear combination in (38).

6.1.4 *Visualization Requirements and Interface*

In the steering environment, the user chooses a parameter μ and is presented in real-time with the visualization of the corresponding full snapshot $\tilde{u}^\mu$. The visualization can be displayed either on a single screen or on several screens attached to several visualization nodes [28]. Recent scientific visualization tends to favor the second scenario. For this, we distribute the repository among the same visu-

6.1 SYSTEM ARCHITECTURE FOR EFFICIENT DATA DELIVERY

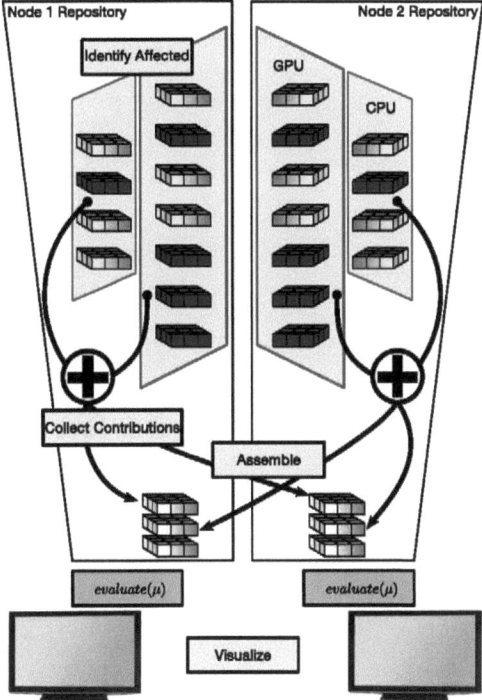

Figure 28: CPU/GPU repository structure with visualization interface. Hierarchized snapshots α_j are distributed among nodes and stored in GPU and main memory. Each repository instance evaluates a part of the final snapshot by identifying the affected blocks (in red) and performing the summation. In order to visualize the full snapshot, the missing slices are gathered from the other nodes.

alization nodes to thus utilize all the available GPUs or main memory. This means each node produces only a slice of the final snapshot. Each visualization node collects all slices with a Message Passing Interface (MPI) *all-gather* operation [88] and renders only the section of the final image corresponding to its view frustum. Note that an explicit *all-gather* operation can be skipped if the visualization environment implements distributed rendering algorithms (classified in [65]).

For the described data delivery, only a minimal interface needs to be exposed by the surrogate implementation to any visualization software. It consists of three methods:

init(): distribute and load the repository,

58   SYSTEM DESIGN

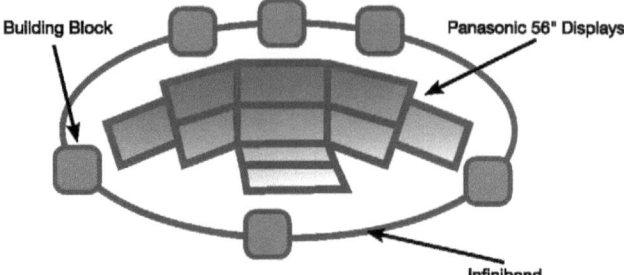

Figure 29: The FRAVE consists of a series of building blocks connected by Infiniband. The current FRAVE setup has 6 building blocks powering 10 displays (8 for the walls, 2 for the floor).

evaluate(μ, buffer): place the full snapshot u^μ in the visualization buffer via all-gather,

improve(μ): trigger several new simulation runs in order to improve the accuracy around μ.

With such an interface, the repository is treated as a pure data deliverer, which stores no information whatsoever about the simulation scenario or its geometry. This allows for loose coupling between components by placing functionality only where it is needed.

6.2 PERFORMANCE

The decisive factor for interactive steering is the performance of the surrogate evaluation. Based on a reference test system which incorporates visualization and computing resources, we next investigate the GPU and GPU-distributed repositories. To better relate to the application, evaluation benchmarks for the NUMA-enhanced CPU version are presented in Sec. 7.5.2, where the BIM application employs such a repository.

The Fully Reconfigurable CAVE Environment (FRAVE) system (see Fig. 29 and [13]) is a multi-display semi-immersive visualization system available at the Technische Universität München. In this thesis, the FRAVE is the target system for a concrete deployment of the repositories and also a reference design for a modern distributed visualization system.

It is organized as a collection of building blocks which enable it to be folded, extended or split up to accommodate a specific type of visualization goal (see Appendix A for detailed information on the FRAVE).

A single building block consists of the following components:

- *Displays*: one or two 3D full HD (1920x1080) 65" plasma screens Panasonic TX-P65VT20E
- *Graphic cards*: an Nvidia QuadroPlex 7000 for graphics (2x 6 GB RAM) and an additional Nvidia Tesla C2070 card (6 GB RAM) for computing purposes
- *Computer*: a dual-socket Intel Xeon E5630 quad-core system (2.53 GHz) with 24 GB RAM and 8 TB hard drive
- *Frame:* a light aluminum frame on which all the above components are mounted and which can be moved freely
- *Inter-connection:* QDR Infiniband network with 32Gbps

Each building block can be added to the system by connecting it to the Infiniband network, when it is needed.

6.2.1 GPU-Based Evaluation and Hierarchization

We first benchmark the *evaluation* as a GPU-local task. This is the actual computation. Second, in case of a GPU-distributed repository, we benchmark also the cost of collecting the full result on each visualization node with an MPI *all-gather* operation.

In the test environment, the repository uses 6 building blocks with all snapshots equally distributed to the 6 instances of the repository. Triggering evaluation on a node implies that only one sixth of a snapshot has to be interpolated. We examine the performance of this operation in two scenarios:

- 200 snapshots, each consisting of $3 \cdot 128^3$ floats (24 MB), total amount of data ≈ 4.8 GB, and
- 150 snapshots, each consisting of $3 \cdot 256^3$ floats (192 MB), total amount of data ≈ 28.1 GB.

The 4.8 GB in the first scenario can also be replicated on all GPU units but then there would be little space left for extending the model through adaptive refinement (as described in Sec. 5.3). The second test scenario aims to put the repository under full load. Figure 30 shows for both scenarios and varying number of affected basis functions (number of SAXPY operations) how long evaluation takes on a single FRAVE node. The chart shows that the repository is able to deliver the partial snapshots well within the response time, even for a larger number of affected basis functions. For smaller numbers of affected basis we can even speak of real-time evaluation. For the sparse

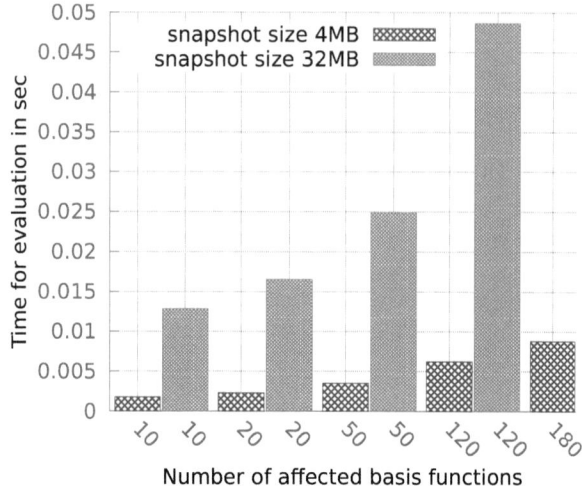

Figure 30: Local evaluation time in two setups with different snapshots sizes: 4 and 32 MB. By extending the model through refinement, the number of affected bases $|A^\mu|$ and thus number of SAXPY operations increases. Even for 120 affected bases of size 32MB the GPU repository delivers real-time results. Due to memory limitations, 180 slices of 32MB don't fit on our test GPU.

grid interpolation only a small subset of snapshots are involved at a time. $|A^\mu|$ is unlikely to exceed 50 in our scenario.

We skip the benchmark of the incremental hierarchization, as the time needed for this operation during the online phase can be approximated. Hierarchization basically corresponds to a number of evaluations executed successively, as sketched in Fig. 27. Multiplying the time for evaluation by k give an estimate of the time needed to add k new snapshots to the surrogate model.

6.2.2 *Data Assembly*

As illustrated in Fig. 28, each node delivers only a slice of a full snapshot $\tilde{u}^\mu(x)$ to the visualization. However, the visualization requires the full snapshot locally in order to render, and a gather step has to be performed. Figure 31 presents the cost of such a gather operation for different node counts and snapshot sizes on the FRAVE's Infiniband network. We notice that the assembly time scales linearly with snapshot size while being almost constant with respect to the

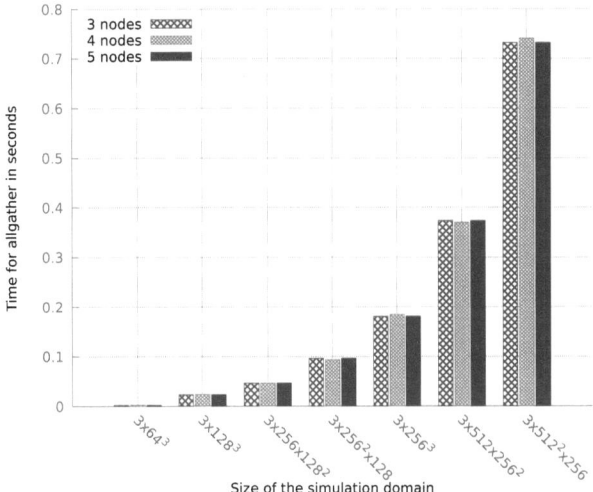

Figure 31: All-gather cost for different snapshot sizes and numbers of nodes. The given spatial resolution refers to the discretization of the domain Ω with three components per discretization node.

number of nodes involved. We do not expect this to be the case for a much higher number of nodes. But for visualization systems like the FRAVE, which consist of a moderate number of nodes, it can be assumed.

While the evaluation achieves a good response time, the assembly costs for snapshots larger than 3×256^3 (192MB) prevent an interactive parameter sweep ($\leqslant 0.2$s). A parameter comparison is however still possible ($\leqslant 2$s). It is worth mentioning that such snapshot sizes are challenging even for classical visualizations and require special approaches to visualize in an interactive manner.

The distributed data availability might actually be more appropriate for distributed visualization algorithms such as parallel volume rendering [100] or distributed streamline computation [71]. In this case the all-gather operation is not needed.

6.2.3 Performance Summary

As expected, the task of summing up weighted large blocks of data is well suited for a high-memory throughput device such as a GPU. The GPU evaluation time for both a large size and count of affected snapshots is below ≈ 0.1 seconds which offers a truly interactive access to interpolated results.

However, if no full replication of the repository is possible, the gather operation – needed to ensure all nodes have the full snapshot – overshadows the efficient evaluation. For snapshots smaller or equal to 3×256^3 floats (192MB) the interactive character is still preserved. Two solutions to reduce the all-gather overhead are possible. First, an overlapping distribution instead of the a disjoint splitting of the repository can be employed. The overlapping pieces would need not be communicated. The second option is to move to a CPU-replicated repository. As we will see in Sec. 7.5.2, in this scenario significantly larger repositories can be fitted in the main memory.

6.3 SUMMARY

In this chapter, we have presented the design and implementation of the sparse grid non-intrusive surrogate model. The repository is a system that stores, constructs, and evaluates the low-fidelity model. All operations performed by the repository are formulated as a series of weighed summations of large vectors (SAXPY operations). This formulation allows a high degree of parallelism which we exploit.

We have developed a GPU repository that streams all snapshots the the GPU and uses SIMT (Single Instruction Multiple Thread) parallelism to speed-up the evaluation. For a large test case with 120 affected snapshots (32MB per snapshot) the GPU-repository performs the evaluation on 0.05sec. Due to its high memory bandwidth, the interpolation requires well below the 0.2sec threshold that marks interactivity.

Memory requirements for the non-intrusive low-fidelity model scale with the number of snapshots considered in its construction and extension. Thus, the amount of memory available on the GPU (currently around 6GB) becomes a limitation for the interpolation of very large snapshots (>128MB). To mitigate this, we have presented a CPU-repository that uses NUMA features for high memory throughput and SIMD parallelism to distribute computation over the available cores. We will evaluate this model in Chap. 7.

7 APPLICATION STEERING

Having introduced the concept of surrogate models for computational steering, we apply it to four applications: a heat conduction problem (thermal block), a shape optimization problem (acoustic horn), the flow through complex geometries (BIM), and a chemical reaction simulation (reactive flow). This short enumeration already suggests a great deal of variety among the applications with respect to the treated physical model, snapshot size, number and type of parameters and even mesh type. The decision to treat such diverse models is not by chance, but aims to show the large applicability of low-fidelity approaches and also different challenges, especially for intrusive models.

The effectiveness of any surrogate model is decided by its two main properties: *accuracy* and *efficiency*. To assess these properties, a scenario will be chosen and presented for each application in detail. For the particular simulation setup the low-fidelity model is constructed in order to benchmark it. Of interest is the accuracy which the surrogate delivers over the parameter domain $\mathcal{P}$. If the accuracy is high enough, then the surrogate becomes useful if it can also deliver new snapshots at interactive rates (it is efficient).

Before applying these criteria to the sparse grid and POD-DEIM low-fidelity models, we shall address some technical aspects regarding the construction of a surrogate from available code or compiled software.

7.1 TECHNICAL ASPECTS

A non-intrusive surrogate model requires the following pieces of information: the size of the discretization domain and the number of stored DoFs per discretization node. Based on this, the total snapshot size is calculated and the repository allocates appropriate storage. Furthermore, a wrapper around the simulation is used to plug in parameter values and trigger simulation runs. The wrapper works with a compiled version of the code and requires no source access whatsoever. Depending on the output format or the output of interest, the obtained snapshots might need some post-processing (e.g, slicing, integration) before they are loaded into the repository.

Many visualization tools have specific internal formats for representing data on grids. The connection between the repository and the visualization component must thus be aware of the used data layout. A non-intrusive model is transparent to the actual format of the data, so a good practice is to store each snapshot in the repository in the same format the visualization expects it. This saves conversion time online, which can be noticeable for large snapshots.

The story is more complicated for intrusive models, where more preparation work is necessary. Access to the source code is needed in order to either modify it or to write a new implementation. In the former case one needs to track down where the large system matrices or states (e.g., initial condition) are assembled. Their reduced versions will then be computed and used instead in the modified algorithm. For solvers which work with full assembled matrices this swap can be easily done. Other solvers that perform grid traversals with local operations need to be rewritten in order to assemble global matrices. These matrices are subsequently reduced, but this workflow of course can require significant implementational effort. In this situation a separate implementation for the low-fidelity model is worth considering.

Another very important aspect for intrusive models is the nature and effect of the parameters on the system of PDE. If a parameter influences a right-hand side term or system matrix entries then the reduction needs to be performed before each run of the low-fidelity model. For repeated usage, this initial reduction significantly limits the efficiency of the surrogate model. Current research efforts to deal with this issue are summed up under the notion of parametrized Model Order Reduction (pMOR). For example, one approach is to interpolate the reduced matrices (see [20, 2, 5]).

As presented in Sec. 5.4, POD-DEIM reduces significantly the cost of evaluating the complete non-linear term. Evaluation only takes place at a smaller set of appropriate DEIM points. However, if the non-linear evaluation at a node has dependencies on neighboring nodes, then these dependencies need to be localized and also computed. One way to automate the identification of the dependencies and the computation of the Jacobian is to use automatic differentiation tools (see [78]), a set of techniques to numerically evaluate the derivative of a function specified by a computer program.

An intrusive model for the reactive flow will be treated in this chapter. Some of the challenges depicted above will be discussed for this specific application, in order to offer a perspective over the implementation efforts.

7.2 EVALUATION CRITERIA

We are first interested in the quality of the achieved approximation within the construction parameter space $\mathcal{P}$. For each simulation a set of test points is used to empirically evaluate the approximation error with the assumption that $\mathcal{P}_s$ is representative for the behavior of the high-fidelity model u.

We distinguish between $\mathcal{P}_s \subset \mathcal{P}$ as the set of parameter combinations samples used to construct the surrogate $\widetilde{u}$, and $\mathcal{P}_t \subset \mathcal{P}$ as the set of parameter combinations used to evaluate the accuracy of $\widetilde{u}$. With $\mathcal{P}_s \cap \mathcal{P}_t = \emptyset$ and N_t as the size of $\mathcal{P}_t$, the approximation error used in the following is given by:

$$\epsilon(\widetilde{u}) = \frac{1}{N_t} \sum_{\mu^* \in \mathcal{P}_t} \|u(\mu^*) - \widetilde{u}(\mu^*)\|_2 \qquad (49)$$

The presented applications are quite different with respect to the number of parameters (2 - 5) and type of parameters (physical and geometrical) but also the number of DoFs per node. For multiple DoFs the error can be computed DoF-wise or aggregated. For some applications (thermal block, acoustic horn) a natural output of interest is defined in the setup of the simulation, and the approximation quality will be given with respect to such an aggregated quantity. Where possible, the relative L_2 error will be preferred.

Second, the efficiency is considered, i.e., the response time within which the surrogate is able to return snapshots for a particular parameter combination. Measurements are presented only for the building infrastructure model (BIM), which due to its large snapshot size (128MB per snapshot) poses challenges for a fast response time. Due to smaller snapshot sizes, the surrogates for all other applications are considered to be interactive. As such, further analysis from this point of view will not be considered.

Finally, through its hierarchical increments and refinement, the sparse grid surrogate model offers knowledge of the behavior of the underlying simulation function. For all applications the visual tools from Sec. 5.2.3 will be evaluated and checked for consistency with known simulation behavior.

7.3 THERMAL BLOCK

The thermal block problem describes the steady-state heat conduction in a square domain consisting of a regular array of 2×2 square

Thermal Block

Characteristic	Value
type	heat transfer
discretization	N = 1056
DoFs/node	1
parameters	conductivities: P_1, P_2, P_3, P_4
parameter type	physical
parameter ranges	$[0.1, 10] \times [0.1, 10] \times [0.1, 10] \times [0.1, 10]$
output of interest	average temperature at top wall

Table 1: Main characteristics of the thermal block problem.

blocks, i.e., regions of different thermal conductivities, see Fig. 32. The problem has four parameters, $\mu \in \mathbb{R}^4$, where each component of μ is the thermal conductivity of one region. The different regions can be considered as different materials which form a composite. On each block we solve:

$$-\mu[i]\Delta u_i = f, \quad i = 1, \ldots, 4 \tag{50}$$

At the top of the domain a non-homogeneous Neumann boundary condition is applied which enforces a uniform flux (unity). The bottom of the domain is cooled to zero by imposing a Dirichlet condition, while the vertical sides are isolated and thus allow for zero flux. Table 1 summarizes the most relevant characteristics for an easy overview. More detailed information for the thermal block is available in [82].

Parameters

The parameters $\mu = \{P1, P2, P2, P4\}$ describe the conductivities of the four sub-domains. A lower conductivity means less heat transport while higher conductivities allow higher heat dissipation. Figure 33 shows a visual depiction of the thermal field for different parameters.

Discretization

The temperature T is discretized on a Cartesian mesh with $N_x \times N_y = 33 \times 32 = 1056$ nodes. At each node a single DoF is stored, namely the temperature.

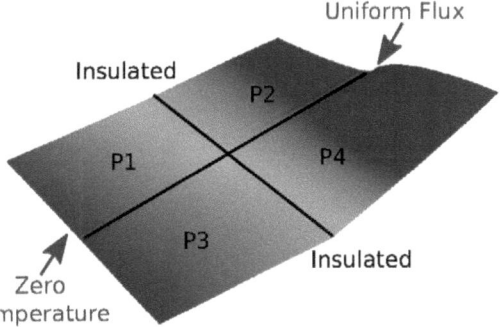

Figure 32: The thermal block investigates heat dissipation through a block of several materials, each with different conductivities μ = [P1, P2, P3, P4].

Output of Interest

The temperature distribution within the whole block is usually of interest, in particular the temperature of the top wall as a function of the block conductivities and conductivity distribution. The top wall temperature can be related to the overall thermal resistance of the domain. A higher resistance means the block acts as an insulator while a low resistance makes the block a good cooling device (transports heat away). For example, the later situation makes the thermal block useful, if it were to be attached to a hot microchip.

Surrogate Model

The sparse grid for the thermal block is four-dimensional and consists of up to $M = 277$ grid points. Such a model size achieves on a test set of size $|P_t| = 10000$ an average L2 error (49) close to 10^{-4} (as shown in Fig. 34). Several points in $\mathcal{P}_t$ have yet to be reached by the refinement process. This causes the maximum error to decrease only slowly with the increase of the sampling size.

Figure 33: Thermal block heat distribution for $\mu = [0.5, 0.5, 0.5, 0.9]$ (left) and $\mu = [0.5, 0.9, 0.5, 0.9]$ (right). A three-dimensional warping of the thermal surface is used to give a better perspective of the temperature differences.

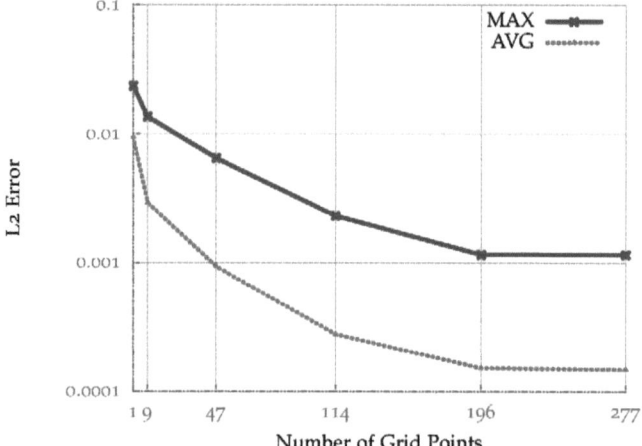

Figure 34: Accuracy of the sparse grid surrogate for the thermal block problem on $|\mathcal{P}_t| = 10000$ test points. With an increasing size of the low-fidelity model, the average L2 error is reduced close to 10^{-4}.

The weighted parallel coordinates plot in Fig. 35 shows interesting insight into the thermal block problem. First, even though the refinement is adaptive, a symmetric refinement pattern with respect to the parameter pairs $[P_1, P_3]$ and $[P_2, P_4]$ can be observed. Such behavior is to be expected as the parameter ranges are identical for the equally-sized sub-blocks. Thus, the conductivity variation due to P_1 should produce the same effect as the one due to P_3. Conductivity changes on the P_2 and P_4 sub-blocks, which are exposed to uniform flux, have also symmetric outcomes (see Fig.32 for the block division).

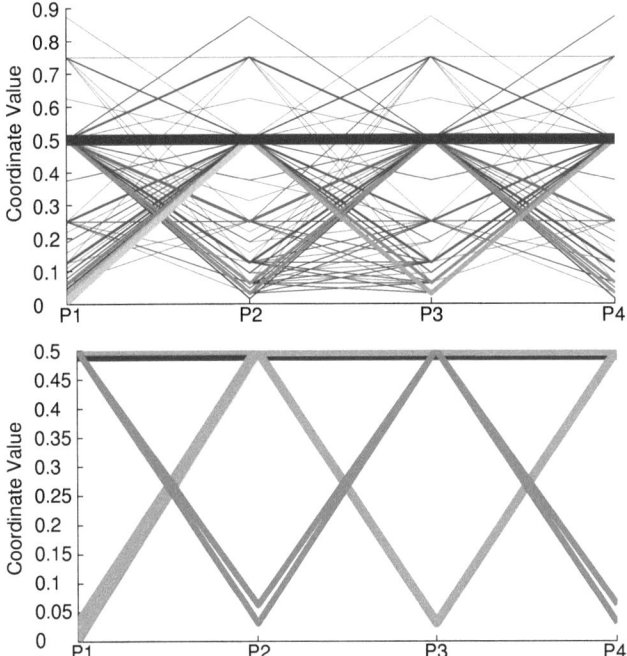

Figure 35: Top: parallel coordinates plot for the thermal block with 277 sparse grid points. Bottom: the same only with the largest contributions. The temperature has a jump at the interface between two neighboring sub-blocks if they are characterized by different conductivities (one conductive while the other less conductive). Such jumps are captured by the refinement and explain why alternating conductivities (e.g, $\mu = [0.0625, 0.5, 0.0625, 0.5]$) have large contributions.

Second, there are some large contributions involving alternating combinations of lower and higher conductivities. Take for example the grid point $\mu = [0.5, 0.0625, 0.5, 0.0625]$. The refinement criteria indicates that a considerable difference in the simulation function is present at this point (relative to other) and a similar one for the reciprocal parameter combination $\mu = [0.0625, 0.5, 0.0625, 0.5]$. If two neighboring nodes correspond to different materials then the coefficient in the heat equation has a jump across the interface. The jump in the conductivity coefficients leads to significant change in the temperature values and this is what the refinement criteria correctly localizes.

The resolution of the high-fidelity model is small. Thus speed up measurements of the low- vs. the high-fidelity one do not make much sense. For this scenario the surrogate is definitely interactive and even for larger three-dimensional thermal blocks we can still expect interactive rates based on the measurements done for the GPU repository for problem independent blocks (see Sec. 6.2).

7.4 ACOUSTIC HORN

The acoustic horn problem consists of a planar channel called the waveguide to which a conical termination called the horn is attached (shown in Fig. 36). An incident wave is generated from the far left of the waveguide and propagated through the horn [4, 26]. In this scenario, of interest is how the shape of the horn influences the wave reflexion back into the waveguide. For various applications a certain shape is desirable so that minimal reflexion is achieved. To obtain different horn designs, its geometry is parametrized at five points along its boundaries (as drawn in Fig. 36). Based on parameter values, a widening or narrowing of the opening of the horn is obtained by local mesh deformations around the chosen nodes. Table 2 summarizes the most important aspects of this scenario.

The acoustic wave equation is used to describe the propagation of sound waves. For sound pressure in one dimension the PDE is formulated as follows:

$$\frac{\Delta^2 P}{\Delta t^2} = c^2 \Delta P, \tag{51}$$

where P is the pressure and c is the speed of sound.

Parameters

The displacements of five points along the horn are to be varied acoording to $\mu = [P0, P1, P2, P3, P4]$. Unlike the thermal block, here the parameters are not of physical nature, but represent geometry changes. No new nodes are added to the mesh by the deformation and no relabeling of the nodes takes place. This means each node can be tracked through different mesh movements.

Discretization

The pressure P is discretized on an unstructured grid with $N = 38967$ nodes (Fig. 36). The deformations represent displacements of existing nodes based on the values of the parameters μ .

7.4 ACOUSTIC HORN

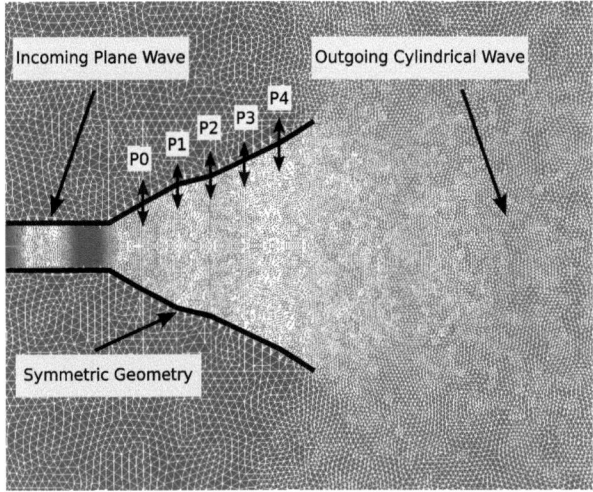

Figure 36: Discretization mesh for the acoustic horn simulation with pressure information. The cone of the horn is deformed at 5 locations. Both walls are deformed symmetrically.

Output of Interest

Of main concern here is usually the optimal shape of the horn that minimizes the acoustic wave reflection back into the waveguide. For our steering purposes, we would like to deform the mesh according to the five displacement parameters and immediately observe the pressure field. Even more, we would like to know which of the parameters or combinations thereof have most impact on the outcome.

Surrogate Model

The sparse grid for the acoustic horn is five-dimensional, where each dimension corresponds to a mesh displacement. For the sparse grid construction, we start with a regular grid of dimensionality three and extend it by adaptive refinement aimed at overall improvement (40). A test set $\mathcal{P}_t$ consisting of 59049 (9^5) parameter combinations sampled on a uniform grid is used for the accuracy investigation. Figure 37 shows the approximation error for test set $\mathcal{P}_t$ with increasing number of points. Interestingly, already the start configuration ($d = 3$) with $M = 71$ grid points achieves a good relative error. Adding

ACOUSTIC HORN	
CHARACTERISTIC	VALUE
type	acoustic wave
discretization	N = 38967, unstructured grid
DOFs/node	1
parameters	displacements: P0, P1, P2, P3, P4
parameter type	geometrical
parameter ranges	[0.7083, 1.1250] × [1.1250, 1.5417] × [1.5417, 1.9583] ×[1.9583, 2.3750] × [2.3750, 2.7917]
output of interest	wave reflection in plane, overall pressure

Table 2: Main characteristics of the acoustic horn problem.

more points reduces only gradually the error which indicates a rather smooth simulation function.

A look at the parallel coordinates plot for the acoustic horn problem in Fig. 39 (left) shows that, unlike for the thermal block, the sparse grid point on level one ($\mu = [0.5, 0.5, 0.5, 0.5, 0.5]$) has the largest contribution to the interpolation. The rest of the points add much smaller contributions. By ignoring the central point and rescaling the remaining hierarchical coefficients (as depicted in Fig. 39 (right)), we observe (relatively) large hierarchical values around the points $[0.5, 0.5, 0.5, 0.5, 0.75]$ and $[0.5, 0.5, 0.5, 0.5, 0.25]$. A snapshot computed for $[0.5, 0.5, 0.5, 0.5, 0.75]$ shows indeed a pressure buildup at the wall of the horn (see Fig. 38 bottom). This justifies the slightly larger surpluses.

Furthermore, a refinement concentration happens in the parameters P_3 and P_4 (as seen in the parallel coordinates plot and also the scatter plot matrix in Fig. 38 top). The simulation function is thus more sensitive to deformations closer to the edge of the horn.

7.5 FLOW THROUGH BUILDING INFRASTRUCTURE

Building Information Models (BIMs) provide a fully detailed product model for constructions, including exact geometric representation and auxiliary information such as material parameters or measured information. Parameter adjustment is also supported in BIM models, which is crucial to the evaluation of buildings, such as an indoor temperature analysis depending on different window and door opening angles and the intensity of the air conditioning system. The goal in the chosen scenario is to examine the flow around and through the

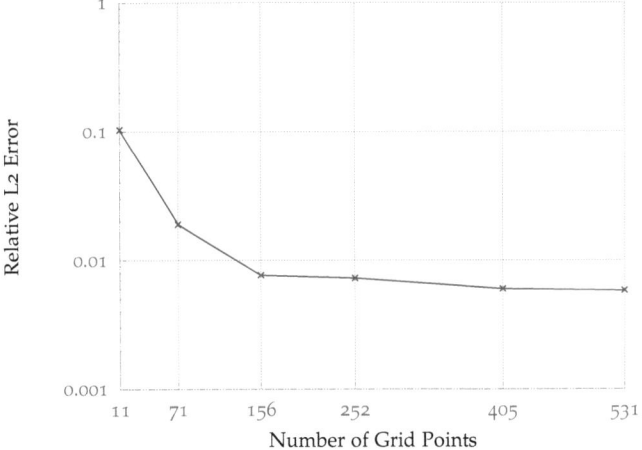

Figure 37: Accuracy of the sparse grid surrogate for the acoustic horn problem.

main building of the Technische Universität München with a special focus set on the influence of several varying parameters. The building's highly detailed model (more than 130k triangles) is obtained by extracting the geometric specification from an Industry Foundation Classes (IFC) [44] product model. Figure 40 provides a visual overview over such an IFC model and highlights the location of two doors, whose opening will be parameterized.

Parameters

A two level parametrization is employed for the BIM flow simulation. The first set of two parameters is used to generate input geometries, which differ in the position of two large doors. Both doors are independently adjusted with opening angles α_1 and α_2 in the range of $[6°; 90°]$. Further parametrization takes place on the simulation level by changing an inflow boundary condition. This third parameter describes the velocity U of a flow that acts perpendicular to the wall with the two doors. U assumes values in [5 m/s; 15 m/s] at the left boundary.

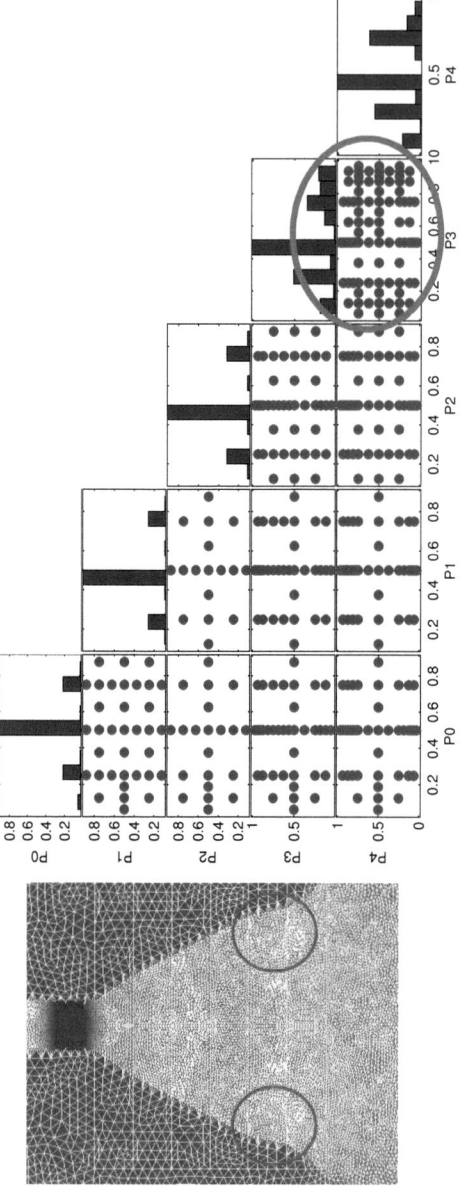

Figure 38: Top: scatter plot matrix for the acoustic horn. The combination of parameters $[P_3, P_4]$ triggers most of the refinement. Bottom: a simulation snapshot for parameters $[0.5, 0.5, 0.5, 0.5, 0.75]$ shows pressure increase towards the wall which motivates the refinement concentration in $[P_3, P_4]$.

7.5 FLOW THROUGH BUILDING INFRASTRUCTURE

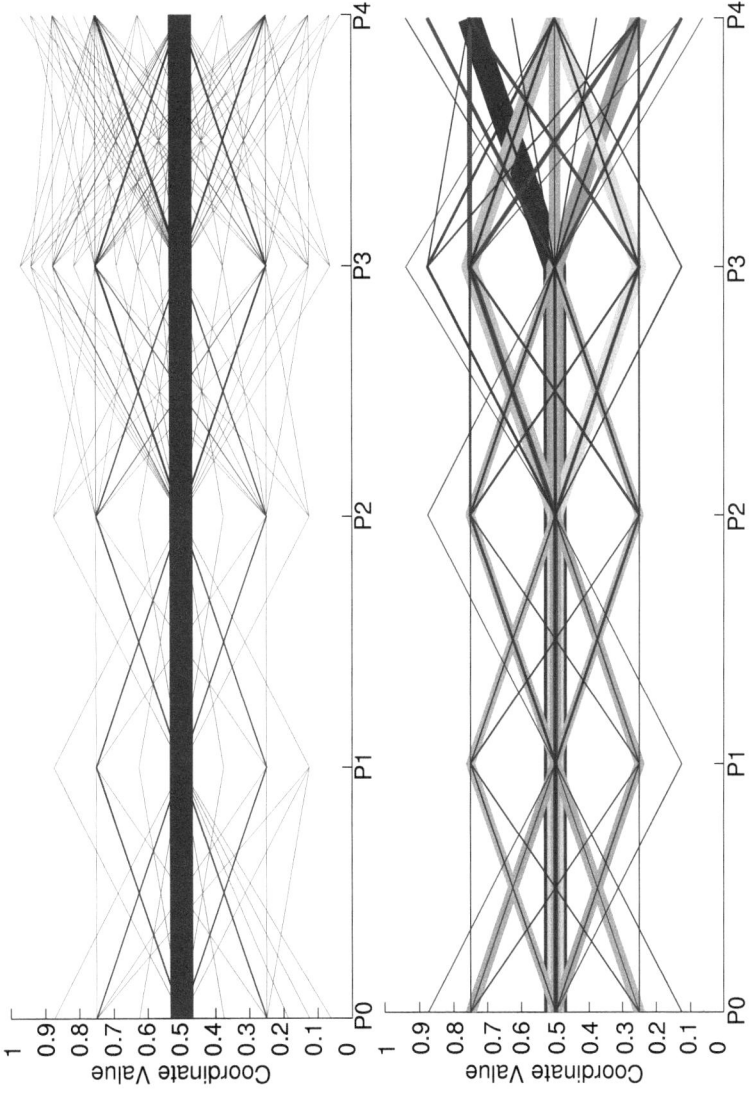

Figure 39: Parallel coordinates plot for the acoustic horn problem (left). Significant refinement is spent for parameters P_3, P_4 indicating sensitivity of the simulation function to this set of parameters. Replotting the parallel coordinates without the central point, reveals several points with larger hierarchical coefficients (right).

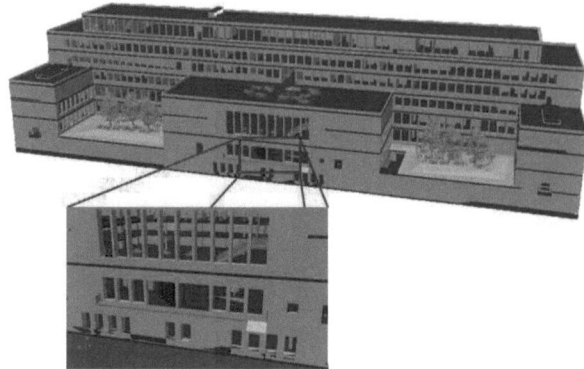

Figure 40: The product model of the central building of the Technische Universität München's main campus. The effect of the opening angle of two central doors (zoom in) is of interest.

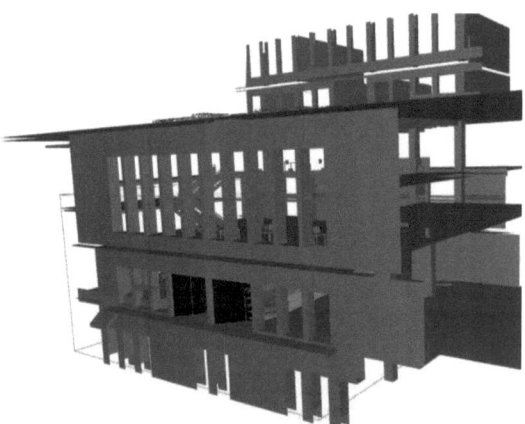

Figure 41: Only the central part of the entire BIM of the main campus is placed in the simulation domain. Furthermore, the surrogate model interpolates only the block of the full simulation domain marked by the red frame. This is motivated by the interest in the flow around the two parametrized doors.

Building Infrastructure Model Flow	
Characteristic	Value
type	potential flow
discretization	$N_x \times N_y \times N_z \times = 1024 \times 256 \times 256$
DOFs/node	4, three velocity components and pressure
parameters	door angles: α_1, α_2, and inflow velocity U
parameter type	geometric and physical
parameter ranges	$[6°, 90°] \times [6°, 90°] \times [5, 15]$ m/s
output of interest	full flow field

Table 3: Main characteristics of the BIM flow simulation.

Discretization

Unlike the acoustic horn where the discretization mesh was deformed based on the parametrization, the BIM flow is discretized on a fixed Cartesian mesh. Changes in door angles correspond to movements of obstacles (the doors themselves) in a fluid domain. Each simulation result is a data block of size $[N_x \times N_y \times N_z \times N_{DOF}] = [1024 \times 256 \times 256 \times 4]$, where N_{DOF} is the number of degrees of freedom per simulation vertex (here: the three components from the velocity field U and the pressure P). The total snapshot size amounts to 1 GB. Note that from the full building in Fig. 40 only the central part is used for the simulation (shown in Fig. 41).

Output of Interest

Changes in the angle of the two doors lead to different flow patterns within rooms of the building. Of interest is not a particular aggregated value but the behavior of the *full* flow with respect to different geometry configurations. To our knowledge, such a requirement makes this simulation a particular challenge for any surrogate modeling method. This is due to the very large size of the snapshot that needs to be interpolated or approximated. The most relevant informations are centralized in Table 3.

7.5.1 *Surrogate Model*

This particular application is part of a larger workflow for taking advantage of detailed building model data (described in Fig. 42). The starting point are complete product model descriptions of construction data, i.e., the fully detailed geometry specification together with auxiliary data such as material parameters and measured information. A set of efficient tools [93, 94] can generate for given parameters and base geometries the corresponding large computational meshes. Computational Fluid Dynamics (CFD) solvers then use the generated discretization to compute a solution snapshot. Note that a second parametrization can also occur on the simulation level. Due to the resolution of the domain, the resulting CFD scenarios are especially challenging and costly to solve. For this scenario the OpenFOAM solver *potentialFOAM* [73] needs ≈ 1 hour per simulation snapshot on the KAUST Shaheen [52] supercomputer. Right now, interactive computational steering is thus only possible with a surrogate model.

As each additional simulation is costly, this particular data fit low-fidelity model needs to be gradually constructed in order to avoid unnecessary high-fidelity evaluations. We thus start to sample the normalized three-dimensional parameter space $\mathcal{P}$, with a small sparse grid of level $l = 3$. This initial model of size $|\mathcal{P}_s| = 31$ is then extended by adaptive refinement.

As the effect of the geometrical changes is local, it makes sense to consider only a part of the full snapshot for investigation. Thus, even though each simulation computes a data block of size $[N_x \times N_y \times N_z \times N_{DOF}] = [1024 \times 256 \times 256 \times 4]$, the surrogate will only work with a slice of each snapshot of dimensions $[512 \times 128 \times 128 \times 4]$ (red frame in Fig. 41), amounting to 128 MB.

Further, we discuss the observed accuracy for the BIM simulation. From a visual point of view, Fig. 43 shows interpolated results for a random parameter combination which match the expected flow behavior. For a quantitative statement we evaluate the surrogate on a test set $\mathcal{P}_t$ constructed by sampling 125 points in a uniform $5 \times 5 \times 5$ grid from the parameter interval $[0.12, 0.92] \times [0.12, 0.92] \times [0.12, 0.92]$.

Before testing for accuracy, $\tilde{u}$ is improved by investing more computational time in the offline phase and thus extending the sparse grid in an adaptive manner. We perform two such extensions by first refining the $l = 3$ model which leads to a surrogate model with $|\mathcal{P}_s| = 77$. A second refinement increases the model size to $|\mathcal{P}_s| = 111$. As expected, we observe an increase in accuracy of the two models over the initial $|\mathcal{P}_s| = 31$ (see Fig. 44). For our defined simulation scenario the sparse grid surrogate can then fulfill its main purpose of being a cheap exploration indicator by delivering a good approximation to the original simulation.

Next, we focus our attention on the visual analytics tools to check if any insight in the BIM simulation can be gained. Figure 46 shows a series of parallel coordinates plots for the different model sizes obtained by refinement. For the smallest (initial) model, the central

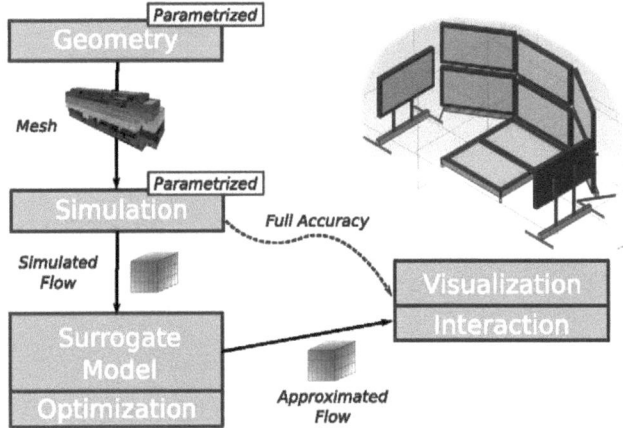

Figure 42: Steering of CFD simulations in accurate building infrastructure models. Such model descriptions give access to a wide number of parameters (material properties, architectural changes) which can be selected for investigation. Geometry changes translate into new computational meshes which are then loaded into the simulation code. At this point, further parametrization is done in the form of boundary conditions. The surrogate model then requires the pre-computation of several full simulations. After construction of the model, approximated results are delivered to the visualization system. Specific to this application, a certain degree of hardware optimization is necessary to deliver interactive data sets.

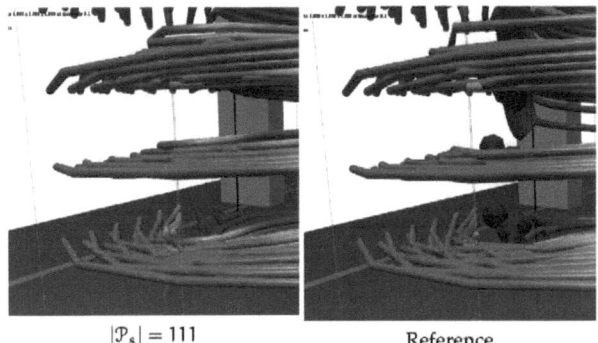

$|\mathcal{P}_s| = 111$ Reference

Figure 43: Left: interpolated flow (zoom in close to the doors) with door angles 32.88° and 83.28° and inflow velocity 12.5m/s. Right: reference solution. With the exception of the immediate vicinity of the door where high-fidelity solution exhibits a slow flow rate (thick blue tubes), the surrogate solution delivers very similar results.

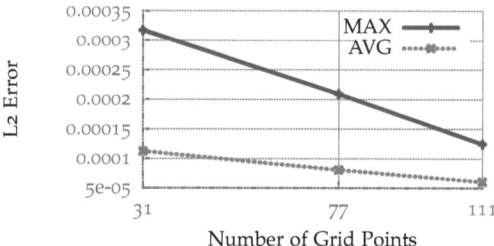

Figure 44: Accuracy of sparse grid surrogates for the BIM problem for surrogate sizes: 31, 77, and 111. For reference, the maximum velocity values are in the range 5-15 m/s.

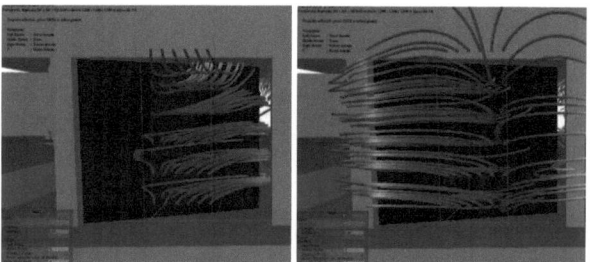

Figure 45: Left: simulation snapshot $\tilde{u}^{[0.5,0.25,0.5]}$. Right: simulation snapshot $\tilde{u}^{[0.5,0.1875,0.5]}$. At a certain closing angle of the door the flow perpendicular to the door no longer passes through but goes around. This large change corresponds to large hierarchical coefficients at neighboring sparse grid points.

7.5 FLOW THROUGH BUILDING INFRASTRUCTURE

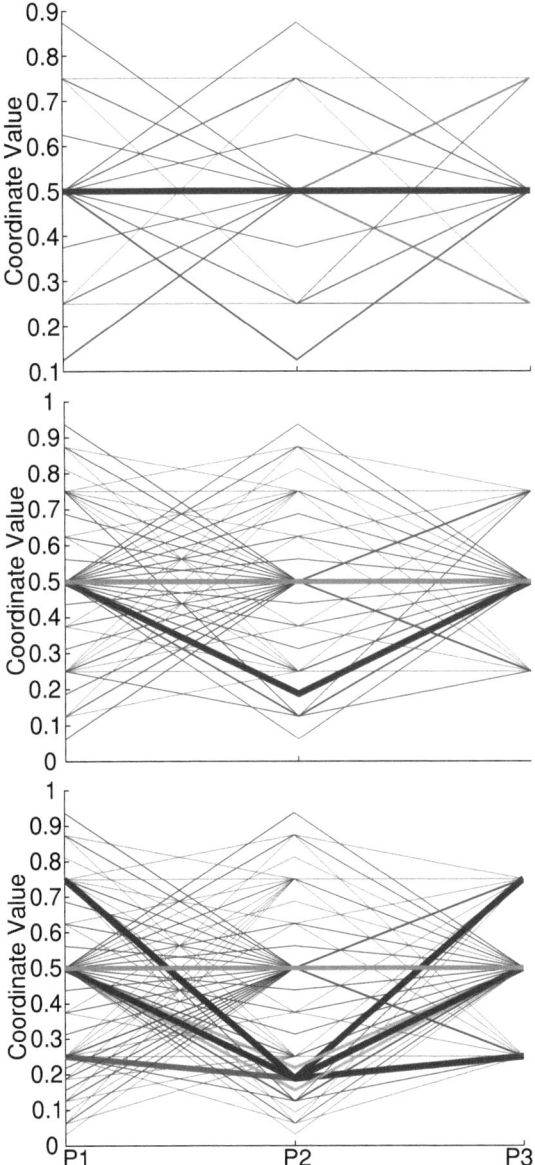

Figure 46: Top: Parallel coordinates plot for a sparse grid with 31 points. Middle: same plot after a refinement which introduces new points. A large hierarchical increment is computed at $\mu = [0.5, 0.1875, 0.5]$ (dark red line). Bottom: a further refinement identifies more points with large contributions around $\mu = [0.5, 0.1875, 0.5]$. The reason for this concentration of significant change is the singularity shown in Fig. 45. Such plots steer the user to interesting behavior.

point has the largest contribution. However, after the first extension a much larger contribution is found at $\mu = [0.5, 0.1875, 0.5]$. A further refinement invests even more points in that area and picks up large contributions. What happens around $[0.5, 0.1875, 0.5]$? A look at snapshots in that area shows indeed a large function change close to the doors. For two simulation snapshots in Fig. 45 at $\mu_1 = [0.5, 0.1875, 0.5]$ and $\mu_2 = [0.5, 0.25, 0.5]$, we observe a large change in the behavior of the flow field. This is caused by the change in the opening angle of the left door (α_2, viewed from outside) which, when almost closed, causes the flow perpendicular to the door to no longer pass through the door but go around it.

The sparse grid surrogate model for the BIM application is very illustrative for how the refinement and the visual tools can identify singularities of a simulation function. Such indicators guide the user to further investigate those areas. This leads to a better understanding of the scenario.

7.5.2 Evaluation Performance

The total size of the repository chosen for the test scenario (128MB×111 ≈ 13.8GB) does fit in the main memory of a single node of the FRAVE test system. As such, we choose the CPU-repository for this application. Each node has a dual-socket NUMA machine with two Intel Xeon E5630 (4 Cores, 12MB cache) clocked at 2.53 GHz. Per node an amount of 24GB of DDR3-1066 RAM is available.

To determine the evaluation time for the BIM scenario, three slices of the simulation domain of sizes 32, 64 and 128 MB were used. The CPU repository loads 111 snapshots of the respective sizes and performs 1000 random evaluations. On average the evaluation involves 23 basis functions ($\approx$ 20 % of the repository).

Figure 47 shows the resulting average evaluation time for different snapshots size with an increasing number of threads. With 8 threads the CPU-repository can perform an evaluation in $\approx$ 200ms. For our steering purpose this qualifies as interactive.

With a full BIM snapshot of 1GB, would the evaluation still be interactive? The decision to pick 1/8 of the full snapshot had to do with our exploration interests. Only the flow around the doors was in focus. Surely, any other part of the domain can be loaded and interpolated just as interactive. However, if the full 1GB snapshots are required then the interactivity would be reduced due the *all-gather* operation needed by the CPU-distributed repository.

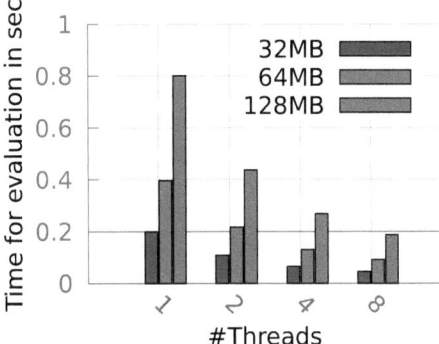

Figure 47: Execution time of the evaluation for different snapshot sizes and for different number of threads on a NUMA machine using the CPU repository with $|\mathcal{P}_s| = 111$. On average 23 affected basis functions were involved in the evaluation.

7.6 REACTIVE FLOW

The reactive flow is a two dimensional H_2-Air flame described by the reaction mechanism $2H_2 + O_2 \rightarrow 2H_2O$, see [9]. A hydrogen and oxygen mix is placed in a rectangular domain and ignited by a flame located at a designated inlet (sketched in Fig. 48). A constant flow is applied from left to right in order to transport the fuel (H_2), oxidizer (O_2), and resulting product (H_2O) through the domain. Due to the convection supplied by the velocity U the reactants leave the domain through the outlet at the far right.

Differential equations that guide the evolution of such flames are non-linear convection-diffusion-reactive equations. For our scenario they take the following form:

$$\frac{\partial x}{\partial t} = \kappa \Delta x - U \nabla x + s(x, \mu) \text{ , in } \Omega. \tag{52}$$

$x(t)$ is the thermo-chemical composition (state) vector that collects all the mass fractions $Y_i \in \mathbb{R}^{N_x \times N_y}$ at each discretization node and the reaction temperature T, thus $x(t) = [Y_1, Y_2, \ldots, Y_{n_s}, T]^T \in \mathbb{R}^N$. For the H_2-Air flame the number of species $n_s = 3$: fuel (F), oxidizer (O), and product (P). For each species $i = F, O, P$, the non-linear reactive source term $s(x, \mu) = [s_1, s_2, \ldots, s_{n_s}, s_T]^T \in \mathbb{R}^N$ is given by:

$$s_i(x, \mu) = -\nu_i \left(\frac{W_i}{\rho}\right) \left(\frac{\rho Y^F}{W_F}\right)^{\nu_F} \left(\frac{\rho Y^O}{W_O}\right)^{\nu_O} A \exp\left(-\frac{E}{RT}\right), \tag{53}$$

REACTIVE FLOW

CHARACTERISTIC	VALUE
type	convection-diffusion-reaction
discretization	$N_x \times N_y = 73 \times 37$
DOFs/node	4 (temperature, fuel, oxidizer, and product)
parameters	activation energy A and pre-exponential factor E
parameter type	physical
parameter ranges	$[5.5^{11}, 1.5^{13}] \times [1.5^3, 9.5^3]$
output of interest	temperature distribution over full domain

Table 4: Main characteristics of the reactive flow problem.

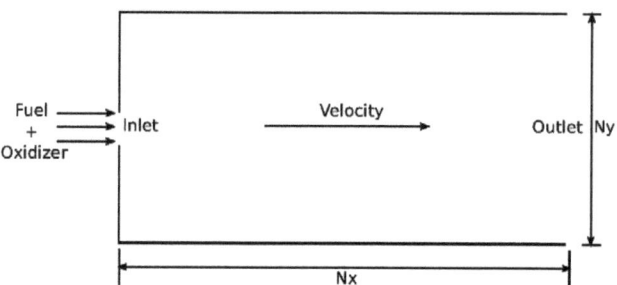

Figure 48: The reactor is a rectangular container with two openings. On the left, through a small opening the fuel and oxidizer are mixed and ignited. A velocity field $\mathcal{U}$ is applied from left to right. The convection transports the reactants and the product out of the domain through the right opening.

where v_i are the respective stoichiometric coefficients, ρ the density of the mixture, and $\mu = (A, E)$ is the vector of parameters. The main characteristics of the simulation scenario are summed up in Table 4.

Parameters

[A, E] form a tuple of physical parameters which influence the reaction rate and are crucial in the study of chemical reactions. The pre-exponential factor A depends on how often molecules collide and on whether the molecules are properly oriented during collision. E is the activation energy, i.e., the minimum energy that must be input to a chemical system with potential reactants in order for a chemical reaction to take place. Different combinations of the two lead to different

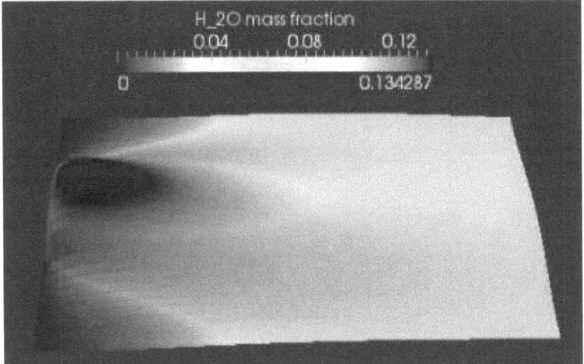

Figure 49: The H_2O concentration plotted with a color mapped height field. The reaction rate has a high value close to the inlet. Convection moves the resulting water throughout the domain.

reaction rates, and, depending on the engineering goal, a minimum or a maximum rate might be searched.

Discretization

Each simulation snapshot is a data block of size $[N_x \times N_y \times N_{DoF}] = [73 \times 37 \times 4]$, where N_{DoF} is the number of degrees of freedom per simulation vertex (here: the fuel H_2, the oxidizer O_2, the product H_2O and the temperature T). Combined, the state vector has size $N = 10804$.

Output of Interest

With three reaction species and the temperature, it is interesting to observe how the different mass fractions change with varying parameters and what role the convection plays. To this purpose a visualization of the full simulation snapshots (see Fig. 49 for an H_2O snapshot) with the possibility of easily changing between the DoFs (H_2O, H_2, O_2 or T) is desired. Of interest are also combinations of A and E that lead to higher temperature development.

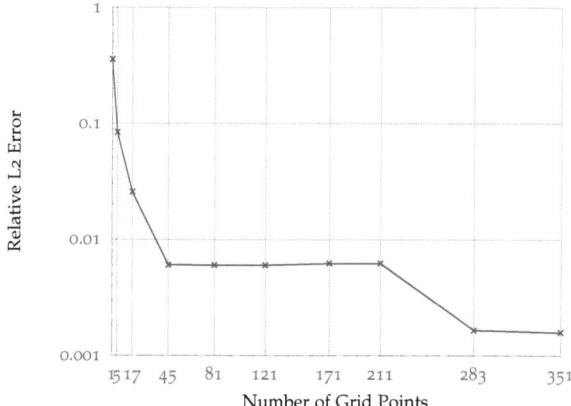

Figure 50: Accuracy of sparse grid surrogates for the reactive flow problem. With M = 45 points a 1% relative L2 error for the temperature T is reached on the test set $\mathcal{P}_t$ consisting of 24x24 uniformly distributed test points.

7.6.1 Non-Intrusive Surrogate

Having only two parameters, this application is rather low dimensional. However, four distinct degrees of freedom per node offer more ways of constructing adaptive surrogate models. Similar to previous workflows, the sparse grid for the reaction flow is constructed with up to 351 points, but based on adaptivity in the T component.

Helpful in understanding this particular simulation scenario is the small number of parameters. With only two we can actually plot the solution at a certain point in the computational grid and see how well the surrogate matches the high-fidelity model. Figure 51 shows the temperature at discretization point $[x, y] = [7, 17]$ over the entire parameter space $\mathcal{P}$. The overall behavior of the temperature is characterized by a steep increase in temperature for a rather narrow A range ($[0 - 0.2]$) followed by an extended saturation phase.

The surrogate model for this application delivers less than one percent relative L2 over a test set of size $|\mathcal{P}_s| = 576$ (see Fig. 50). At $[x, y] = [7, 17]$, the response surface that the surrogate delivers, closely matches the true behavior of the simulated temperature values (compare Fig. 52 with the true solution in Fig 51). Some error towards the $A = 0$ region of steep function change (Fig. 53) can be observed.

7.6 REACTIVE FLOW   87

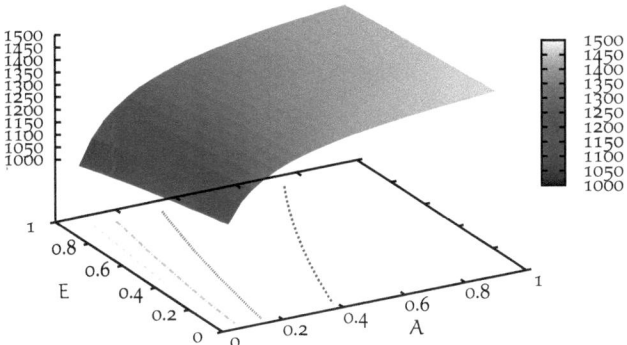

Figure 51: Actual temperature at discretization point $[x, y] = [7, 17]$ over the entire parameter domain $\mathcal{P}$. The activation energy E has rather moderate influence on the reaction temperature. The increase in temperature is mostly caused by an increase in the rate of molecule collisions A.

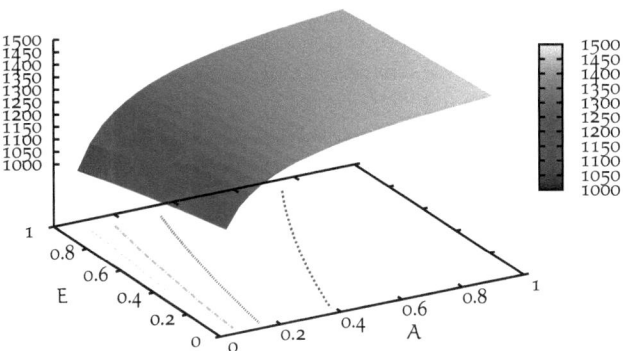

Figure 52: Approximated temperature at discretization point $[x, y] = [7, 17]$ over the entire parameter domain $\mathcal{P}$. The surrogate matches well the overall behavior of the true solution.

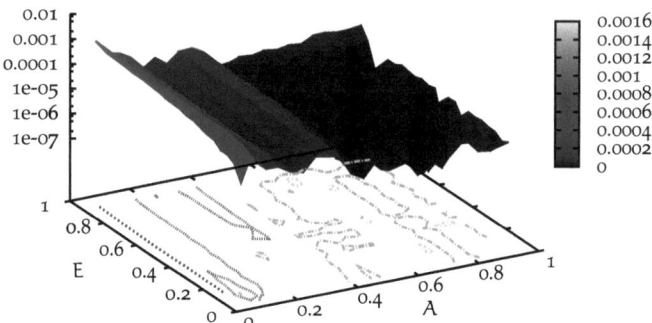

Figure 53: Relative error for temperature at discretization point $[x,y] = [7,17]$ over the parameter domain $\mathcal{P}$.

Next, we turn to the visual analytics based on the hierarchical increments in order to see if the actual simulation function in Fig. 51 can also be hinted from the refinement and magnitude of the α_i.

First, the scatter plot matrix for this application is changed by resizing the points based on the corresponding $|\alpha_i|$. From the (scaled) scatter plot matrix in Fig. 54 we observe that a large hierarchical coefficient corresponds to the central point $[0.5, 0.5]$ and significant corrections are applied especially to the left towards $A = 0$. This indeed hints the behavior of the simulation function which exhibits a steep decrease in the same direction.

Second, from the parallel coordinates plot in Fig. 55, we can also observe very easily that refinement mostly focuses on the pre-exponential factor A. The simulation is thus most sensible to this parameter, and, more precisely, in a particular A range $[0-0.25]$ the sensitivity gradient is particularly high.

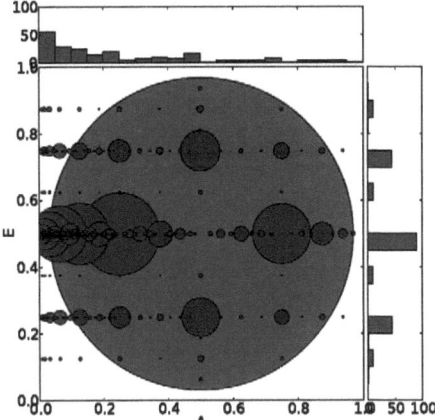

Figure 54: Scatter plot for the reaction flow where each sparse grid point is scaled by the size of its increment. The central point $\mu = [0.5, 0.5]$ contributes most to the interpolation. The refinement focuses very well on the change in the function towards $A = 0$ (compare to Fig. 51).

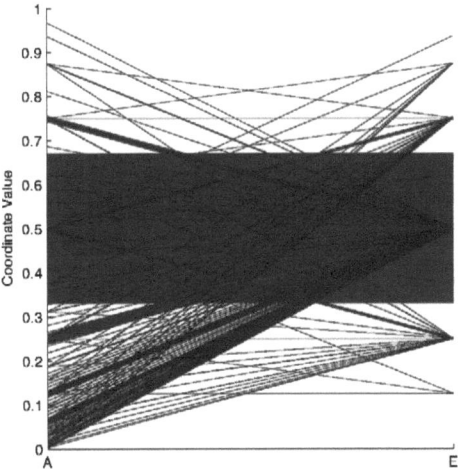

Figure 55: Parallel coordinates for the reaction flow example. We see a clear refinement concentration over the whole range of the activation energy A, but especially in the interval $[0, 0.25]$.

We conclude from the investigation of the reactive flow that the sparse grid surrogate model fulfills both aims of simulation exploration. Not only can new snapshots be extracted at interactive rates but the underlying structure of the surrogate model gives valuable insight (similar to sensitivities) in the actual reaction behavior.

7.6.2 Intrusive Surrogate

With the PDE at hand, the construction of the intrusive POD-DEIM surrogate involves quite a few steps. At this point, the computation of the orthonormal basis V has already been performed (as presented in Sec. 5.4). With V, the state vector, convection, and diffusion matrices are brought to their reduced versions through projections of the form $V^T x(t,p)$ and $V^T A V$ respectively.

After the linear reduction is in place, attention now moves to the non-linear reaction term. The classical DEIM method computes a second set of orthonormal basis U and a row selection matrix P which are used to interpolate the non-linear term. As a result the reaction term is also reduced by requiring non-linear evaluations only at the vertices selected by P:

$$V^T s(x, \mu) \approx \underbrace{V^T U (P^T U)^{-1}}_{pre-computed} s(\underbrace{Px}_{reduction}, \mu) \tag{54}$$

In Sec. 5.4 an improved version of the classical DEIM has been presented that uses DEIM residual-based clustering. Instead of a single global basis V and a selection matrix P, a collection of bases V_k and corresponding projection matrices P_k is used to better capture the non-linearity.

The precomputed clustering in the parameter domain (spanned by A and E) is used to build a classification function $c : \mathcal{P} \longrightarrow k$. For a given start parameter combination c, maps the parameter tuple [A, E] to an appropriate cluster number k associated with a tuple $[U_k, P_k]$. Having made this choice, the solving proceeds as usual with this improved interpolation of the reaction term.

Similar to a non-intrusive method, a construction $\mathcal{P}_s$ and test $\mathcal{P}_t$ set of snapshots is used to compute the accuracy of the surrogate. For the reactive flow, $\mathcal{P}_s$ and $\mathcal{P}_t$ are both uniform samplings of $\mathcal{P}$ with a 50x50 and 24x24 resolution respectively. Of interest is the improvement in error in the temperature component due to the use of localized DEIM.

First of all, does clustering also deliver meaningful results for the reactive flow? Figure 56 (top) and 57 (top) present the results of a parameter clustering for $k = 10$ and $k = 25$. A quick look at the shape of the non-linear term (see Fig. 51) does indeed confirm that the computed clusters do represent areas of similar function behavior. Note that a static initialization (vertical stripes) of the clusters has been used for stability reasons.

Next, does the localized basis selection improve the overall accuracy for the reactive flow? Figure 56 (bottom) 57 (bottom) show that up to two digits (e.g., $k = 10, n_{POD} = 20, n_{DEIM} = 20$) in accuracy can be gained over the classical DEIM by taking advantage of locality.

Discussion

As with the two peak function (see Sec. 5.4), the reduced model of the reactive flow also profits from DEIM locality. The gain can be seen from two points of view. On one side, LDEIM delivers improved accuracy for the same number of DEIM points. This is particularly useful if the number of DEIM points in the classical method cannot be increased due to computational constraints. On the other side, and this brings us closer to computational steering demands, LDEIM offers similar accuracy for a smaller number of non-linear term evaluations. The reduction in DEIM points speeds up the evaluation of the reduced model so that interactivity or even real-time responses are possible.

Besides the query of the map c at simulation start, the computational costs in the online phase are unchanged to the classic DEIM. Solely the offline phase becomes more expensive as it involves the repeated computation of several DEIM bases, albeit of smaller size.

There are limits to the desired number of clusters k. For the reactive problem, an increase in the number of clusters from 10 to 25 does not bring significant improvement. The main separable features of the non-linear function have already been well captured with fewer clusters.

7.7 SUMMARY

In this chapter, we have presented the accuracy of the non-intrusive sparse grid surrogates of four applications. With a moderate number of construction samples (<500) an average relative L2 error of 1% or less has been obtained. For the purpose of visual computational steering such an error threshold captures the global behavior of the underlying simulation.

Furthermore, by inserting the hierarchical coefficients into visual analytics tools we gained insight into parameter sensitivity. For the

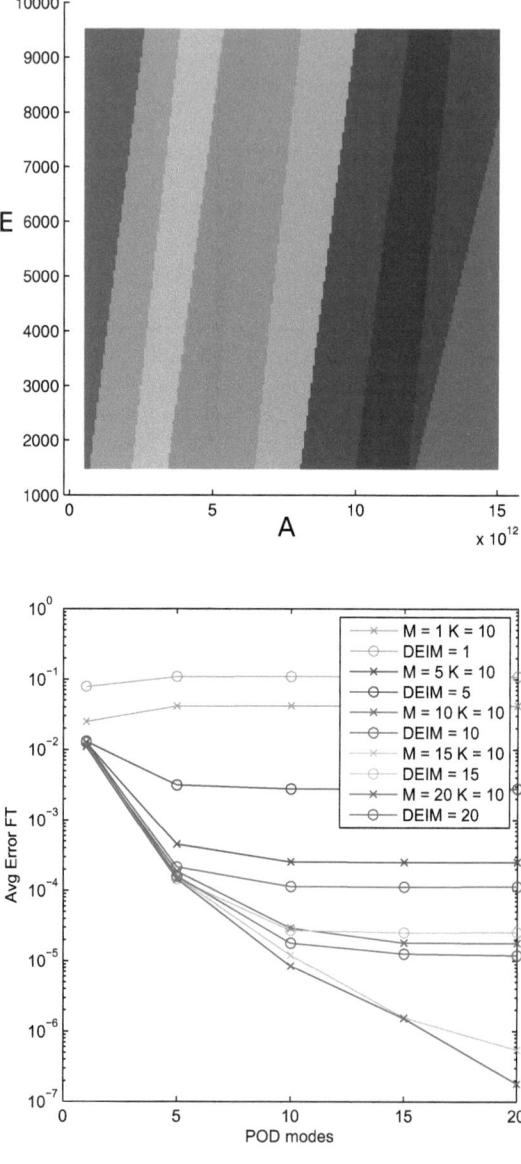

Figure 56: Top: residual-based parameter space clustering with $k = 10$. Bottom: error comparison between classical vs localized DEIM for an increasing number of DEIM points (n_{DEIM}). On the horizontal axis the number of global POD modes is increased (n_{POD}).

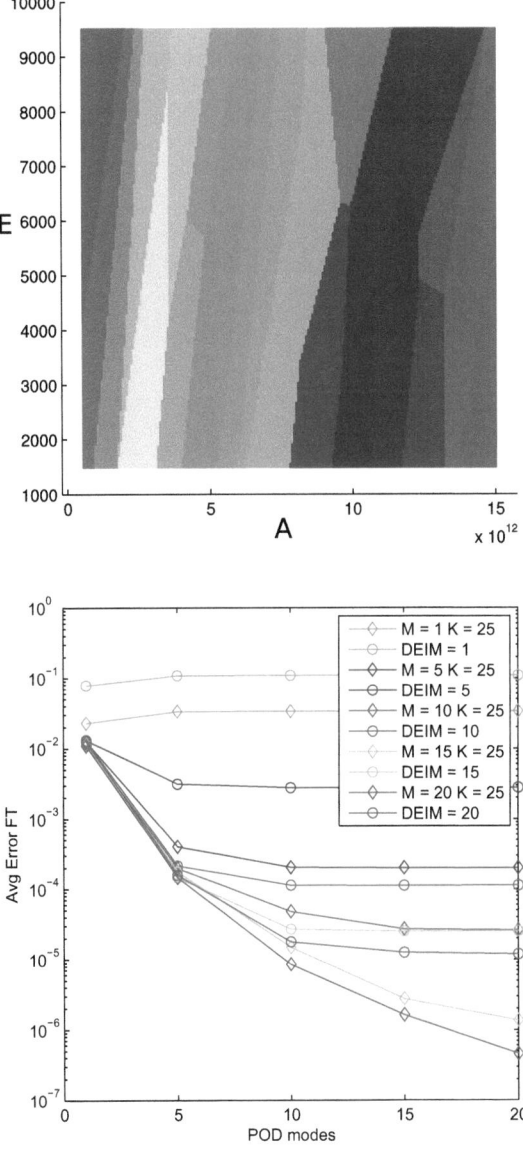

Figure 57: Top: residual-based parameter space clustering with k = 25. Bottom: error comparison between classical vs localized DEIM for an increasing number of DEIM points (n_{DEIM}). On the horizontal axis the number of global POD modes is increased (n_{POD}).

thermal block, an alternating combination of high and low parameter combinations leads to jumps in the temperature distribution. The acoustic horn has a rather smooth parameter response but some areas of pressure buildup have been visually identified. The BIM simulation had a particular singularity at $\mu_1 = [0.5, 0.1875, 0.5]$ caused by the closing of one of the doors. The reactive flow is more sensitive to the parameter A than E. Even narrower, for values closer to the lower range of A significant change in the temperature behavior has been identified.

On the intrusive track, the POD-LDEIM surrogate for the reactive flow has improved the accuracy of the classical DEIM method with up to two digits.

CONCLUSIONS

Classical computational steering approaches have been tackling the lack of interactivity of complex applications by employing either parallel architectures, or, similar in the spirit of this thesis, making computational simplifications by running simulations mainly with lower resolutions. The main contribution of this thesis is to push this idea even further, by formulating an extension of the notion of computational steering to include an approximation layer. Built with computational effort invested ahead of the actual steering process, this layer delivers approximate, but interactive results. A smooth steering experience becomes possible where before was not the case. When used for what-if or sensitivity analyses, such an extension significantly speeds up the time to results by reducing the number of expensive high-fidelity simulations needed to understand the effect of parameters in a certain simulation scenario.

As approximation layers, this work contributes data fit and reduced order surrogates, which reduce the computational complexity of several parametrized simulations described by partial differential equations. In what-if analysis, for which the qualitative behavior of the simulation is sufficient to draw conclusions, sacrificing some accuracy for interactivity has proven to be a viable alternative.

A successful use of low fidelity models for steering depends on two criteria, namely, their accuracy and response time. On a set of four applications consisting of a thermal block, an acoustic horn, a flow through accurate building structures, and a reactive flow, the nonintrusive adaptive sparse grid surrogate model achieves an average L_2 error around 1 per cent within the targeted parameter ranges and for the defined scenarios. Such an error threshold is sufficient to assess simulation snapshots in a visualization system. Of course, reaching this target of 1 per cent error required a different number of training snapshots, depending on the smoothness of the simulation function under consideration. For strongly varying simulation functions, it is imaginable that the number of snapshots needed to reach the accuracy threshold can increase significantly.

On a parallel track, the reactive flow has additionally been treated with an intrusive surrogate model based on POD-DEIM. This thesis contributes an extension to the classical DEIM by a parameter space clustering approach, which is better suited for problems with nonlinearities that exhibit separable features. An improvement of up to two digits in accuracy over the classical DEIM is achieved. The intrusive surrogate shows for the reactive flow superior accuracy to its non-intrusive counterpart, but comes with the price of significant changes in the original system of differential equations.

With 0.2ms as the upper time limit for an evaluation of the low-fidelity model, a non-intrusive repository concept has been developed that efficiently delivers new snapshots. Several versions have been implemented and tested: a GPU, a GPU-distributed, and a CPU-based repository, each suited for different problem sizes and available resources. Regarding efficiency, the BIM (flow through complex geometries) application was the most challenging one, with individual snapshots measuring 128MB. Making efficient use of NUMA CPU architecture, the repository was able to deliver new snapshots within the upper limit.

The entire steering process with surrogate models is seen as a continuous exploration process. Although the number of parameters targeted by the presented methods is rather moderate (2-10) there is still a large parameter space to search. Hierarchical coefficients and refinement patterns employed by the sparse grid surrogate proved capable in identifying important parameters, parameter combinations, and parameter ranges. Furthermore, the repository has been designed to be extensible during the online phase. Automatically or triggered by user demand, new simulation results improve the solution during exploration.

The fact that the response of simulations to parameter changes can be approximated by simpler models or that large discretizations can be reduced to a mere fraction of their original computational cost, indicates a lot of redundancy and thus potential to bring down the cost or frequency of simulations. There are of course a series of open questions. For example, regarding only stationary solutions, the considered applications did not involve time as a parameter. While the sparse grid surrogate can consider time as just another parameter, for oscillating snapshots trajectories, this might not be appropriate. The POD-DEIM does not have this issue, but its reduction potential depends on the data dependencies in the non-linear term. At the same time, the implementation efforts of an intrusive low-fidelity model are not negligible.

As demonstrated, surrogates significantly contribute to advances in interactive prototyping and visual based understanding of complex parameterized simulation scenarios.

VISUAL ENVIRONMENT

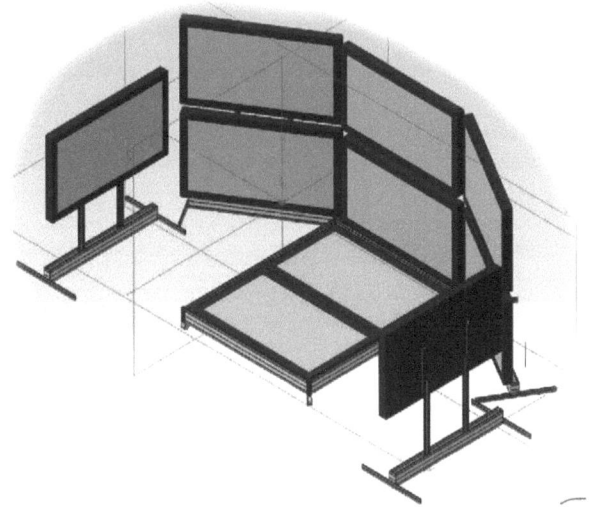

Figure 58: FRAVE – The Fully Reconfigurable CAVE Environment. Motivated by the concept of the CAVE [19] as an immersive virtual reality environment, the main design idea behind the FRAVE is its modularity. A FRAVE module consists of a display unit together with a compute unit mounted on a common aluminum frame. The display consists of one (sides) or two (center and floor) plasma screens (Panasonic TX-P65VT20E) with full-HD resolution and 3D capabilities. A workstation (dual-socket Intel Xeon E5630 quad-core, 24 GB RAM and 8 TB hard drive) attached to the frame of each module offers resources for visualization or computation. An external GPU (Nvidia QuadroPlex 7000) is connected to each workstation to power the displays. A second internal GPU (Nvidia Tesla C2070) is reserved for compute intensive tasks. Each module can be freely moved to fit different visualization purposes, e.g, a flat surface for high-resolution 2D visualization or closed for immersive 3D environments.

Figure 59: FRAVE displaying the BIM application. The visualization of the BIM model and fluid flow is distributed across the displays using the Equalizer library [28]. For flow visualization the concept of probes (blue cube) is used. Each probe seeds a number of particles or streamlines and can be easily moved and placed in areas of interest (next to the door in the image).

Summed up below is the detailed description of the FRAVE system.

6x Building block

- 2x (resp. 1x) Panasonic TX-P65VT20E, 65" Full HD, 120 fps (60 HZ for 3D)
- 2x Intel Xeon E5630, (4 Core, 12M cache, 2,53 GHz)
- 2x 12 GB EEC DDR3-1066 RAM
- 1x Nvidia Tesla C2070 (15 SP, 6 GB RAM)
- 1x Nvidia Quadroplex 7000 (2x16 SP, 2x6 GB RAM)
- 1x Mellanox Connect-X2 VPI HCA (32 Gbps IB or 10Gbps ET)

3x Post-processing nodes

- IBM x3550 M3 Server Blade
- 2x Intel Xeon X5690, (6 Core, 12M cache, 3,46GHz)

- 2x 48 GB ECC DDR3-1333 RAM
- 1x Mellanox Connect-X2 VPI HCA (32Gbps IB or 10Gbps ET)

Infiniband network

- 2x Switch Mellanox IS5030 for 1410 36-Port Managed QDR IB
- 2.88 Tbps switching capacity
- 36 ports with 32 Gbps per port
- 9x HCA Card: Mellanox Connect-X2 VPI HCA

User interaction

- 3D viewing via Active Shutter Technology
- rigid body tracking with 8x OptiTrack S250e infrared cameras
- Phantom Premium 6 DOF Haptic Device
- 5DT Data Glove Ultra
- Microsoft Kinect and mobile devices

B

DEIM ENRICHMENT

To avoid discontinuities on the border between two clusters, an overlap is added. A local DEIM basis is thus built from the SVD of the matrix of snapshots in that particular cluster, but with added snapshots from neighboring clusters. Let us consider the snapshots associates with two clusters arranged in the matrices

$$X_1 = \begin{bmatrix} | & & | & | & | \\ x_1 & \cdots & x_{t-2} & x_{t-1} & x_t \\ | & & | & | & | \end{bmatrix}, X_2 = \begin{bmatrix} | & & | & | \\ x_1 & \cdots & x_{s-1} & x_s \\ | & & | & | \end{bmatrix}. \tag{55}$$

The order of the columns in X_1, X_2 corresponds to a decreasing DEIM residual (47), i.e, the last columns have the largest DEIM residual and are thus least well represented by the local DEIM basis. These snapshots are used to enrich neighboring DEIM bases. We pick the last 10% of each X_i and assign it to the local basis with the lowest DEIM residual (excluding their current basis). The first clustering then contains

$$X_1 = \begin{bmatrix} | & & | & | & | & | & | \\ x_1 & \cdots & x_{t-2} & x_{t-1} & x_t & x_{s-1} & x_s \\ | & & | & | & | & | & | \end{bmatrix}, \tag{56}$$

and the second

$$X_2 = \begin{bmatrix} | & & | & | & | & | & | \\ x_1 & \cdots & x_{s-1} & x_s & x_{t-2} & x_{t-1} & x_t \\ | & & | & | & | & | & | \end{bmatrix}. \tag{57}$$

The local DEIM bases are then computed from the SVD of X_i. Note that the classification remains unchanged, i.e., a snapshot belongs to a single cluster. The presented enrichment is only involved with the construction of the DEIM bases.

BIBLIOGRAPHY

[1] V. Algazi and D. Sakrison. On the optimality of the karhunen-loève expansion (corresp.). *Information Theory, IEEE Transactions on*, 15(2):319–321, 1969.

[2] D. Amsallem and C. Farhat. An online method for interpolating linear parametric reduced-order models. *SIAM Journal on Scientific Computing*, 33(5):2169–2198, January 2011.

[3] D. Amsallem, M. J. Zahr, and C. Farhat. Nonlinear model order reduction based on local reduced-order bases. *International Journal for Numerical Methods in Engineering*, 92(10):891–916, December 2012.

[4] E. Baengtsson, D. Noreland, and M. Berggren. Shape optimization of an acoustic horn. *Computer Methods in Applied Mechanics and Engineering*, 192(11–12):1533–1571, 2003.

[5] U. Baur, C. Beattie, P. Benner, and S. Gugercin. Interpolatory projection methods for parameterized model reduction. *SIAM Journal on Scientific Computing*, 33(5):2489–2518, 2011.

[6] N. Bell and M Garland. Efficient sparse matrix-vector multiplication on CUDA. NVIDIA Technical Report NVR-2008-004, NVIDIA Corporation, December 2008.

[7] M. Berveiller, B. Sudret, and M. Lemaire. Stochastic finite element: a non intrusive approach by regression. *European Journal of Computational Mechanics/Revue Européenne de Mécanique Numérique*, 15(1-3):81–92, 2006.

[8] J. Biddiscombe, J. Soumagne, G. Oger, D. Guibert, and J.-G. Piccinali. Parallel computational steering and analysis for hpc applications using a paraview interface and the hdf5 dsm virtual file driver. In *Proceedings of the 11th Eurographics conference on Parallel Graphics and Visualization*, EG PGV'11, pages 91–100, 2011.

[9] M. Buffoni and K. Willcox. Projection-based model reduction for reacting flows. In *40th Fluid Dynamics Conference and Exhibit*, 2010.

[10] H.-J. Bungartz and M. Griebel. Sparse grids. *Acta Numerica*, 13: 147–269, 2004.

[11] S. Burrows, B. Stein, J. Frochte, D. Wiesner, and K. Müller. Simulation data mining for supporting bridge design. In *Proceedings of the 11th AusDM*, 2011.

[12] G. Buse, R. Jacob, D. Pflüger, and A. Murarasu. A non-static data layout enhancing parallelism and vectorization in sparse grid algorithms. In *Proceeding of the 11th International Symposium on Parallel and Distributed Computing - ISPDC 2012*. IEEE, June 2012.

[13] D Butnaru, D. Pflüger, and H.-J. Bungartz. A parallel and distributed surrogate model implementation for computational steering. In *Proceeding of the 11th International Symposium on Parallel and Distributed Computing - ISPDC*. IEEE, 2012.

[14] S. Chaturantabut. *Nonlinear Model Reduction via Discrete Empirical Interpolation*. PhD thesis, Rice University, 2011.

[15] S. Chaturantabut and D. Sorensen. Nonlinear model reduction via discrete empirical interpolation. *SIAM Journal on Scientific Computing*, 32(5):2737–2764, 2010.

[16] S. Chaturantabut and D. C. Sorensen. A state space error estimate for pod-deim nonlinear model reduction. *SIAM Journal on Numerical Analysis*, 50(1):46–63, 2012.

[17] W. S Cleveland and R. McGill. The many faces of a scatterplot. *Journal of the American Statistical Association*, 79(388):807–822, 1984.

[18] T. Crestaux, O. Le Maitre, and J.-M. Martinez. Polynomial chaos expansion for sensitivity analysis. *Reliability Engineering & System Safety*, 94(7):1161–1172, 2009.

[19] C. Cruz-Neira, D. J. Sandin, T. DeFanti, V. R. Kenyon, and J. C. Hart. The cave: audio visual experience automatic virtual environment. *Commun. ACM*, 35(6):64–72, June 1992.

[20] J. Degroote, J. Vierendeels, and K. Willcox. Interpolation among reduced-order matrices to obtain parameterized models for design, optimization and probabilistic analysis. *Int. J. Numer. Meth. Fluids*, 63(2):207–230, 2010.

[21] Q. Du and M. D. Gunzburger. Centroidal voronoi tessellation based proper orthogonal decomposition analysis. *Control and estimation of distributed parameter systems*, pages 137–150, 2003.

[22] J. Eftang and B Stamm. Parameter multi-domain hp empirical interpolation. *International Journal for Numerical Methods in Engineering*, 90(4):412–428, April 2012.

[23] J. Eftang, A. Patera, and E. Rønquist. An hp certified reduced basis method for parametrized elliptic partial differential equations. *SIAM Journal on Scientific Computing*, 32(6):3170–3200, January 2010.

[24] J. Eftang, D. J. Knezevic, and A. T. Patera. An hp certified reduced basis method for parametrized parabolic partial differential equations. *Mathematical and Computer Modelling of Dynamical Systems*, 17(4):395–422, July 2011.

[25] J. Eftang, A. Patera, and E.M. Rønquist. An hp certified reduced basis method for parametrized parabolic partial differential equations. In *Spectral and High Order Methods for Partial Differential Equations*, volume 76, pages 179–187. 2011.

[26] J. L. Eftang, D. B. P. Huynh, D. J. Knezevic, and A. T. Patera. A two-step certified reduced basis method. *Journal of Scientific Computing*, 51(1):28–58, 2012.

[27] T. Eickermann, W. Frings, and A Visser. Visit – a visualization interface toolkit. Technical report, Tech. Rep. Central Insitute for Applied Mathematics, 2000.

[28] S. Eilemann, M. Makhinya, and Renato Pajarola. Equalizer: A scalable parallel rendering framework. *Visualization and Computer Graphics, IEEE Transactions on*, 15(3):436–452, 2009.

[29] M. S. Eldred. Recent Advances in Non-Intrusive Polynomial Chaos and Stochastic Collocation Methods for Uncertainty Analysis and Design. In *Structures, Structural Dynamics, and Materials Conference*, May 2009.

[30] M. S. Eldred and J. Burkardt. Comparison of non-intrusive polynomial chaos and stochastic collocation methods for uncertainty quantification. volume 123, 2009.

[31] M. S. Eldred and D. M. Dunlavy. Formulations for surrogate-based optimization with data-fit, multifidelity and reduced-order models. In *Proceedings of the 11th AIAA/ISSMO Multidisciplinary Analysis and Optimization Conference*, 2006.

[32] N. Fabian, K. Moreland, D. Thompson, A.C. Bauer, P. Marion, B. Geveci, M. Rasquin, and K.E. Jansen. The paraview coprocessing library: A scalable, general purpose in situ visualization library. In *Large Data Analysis and Visualization (LDAV)*, pages 89–96, 2011.

[33] M. Frangos, Y. Marzouk, K. Willcox, and B. van Bloemen Waanders. *Surrogate and Reduced-Order Modeling: A Comparison of Approaches for Large-Scale Statistical Inverse Problems*, pages 123–149. John Wiley & Sons, Ltd, 2010.

[34] C.H. Frey and S. R. Patil. Identification and Review of Sensitivity Analysis Methods. *Risk Analysis*, 22(3):553–578, 2002.

[35] I. J. Geist, G. A. Geist, J. Ii, A. Kohl, and P. M. Papadopoulos. Cumulvs: Providing fault-tolerance, visualization and steering of parallel applications. *International Journal of High Performance Computing Applications*, 11:224–236, 1996.

[36] A. A. Giunta, S. F. Wojtkiewicz, and M. S. Eldred. Overview of modern design of experiments methods for computational simulations. In *Proceedings of the 41st AIAA Aerospace Sciences Meeting and Exhibit, AIAA-2003-0649*, 2003.

[37] G. Golub and W. Kahan. Calculating the Singular Values and Pseudo-Inverse of a Matrix. *Journal of the Society for Industrial and Applied Mathematics, Series B: Numerical Analysis*, 2(2):205–224, 1965.

[38] G.H. Golub and C.F. Van Loan. *Matrix Computations*. Johns Hopkins Studies in the Mathematical Sciences. Johns Hopkins University Press, 1996.

[39] T. Goodale, G. Allen, G. Lanfermann, J Massó, T. Radke, E. Seidel, and J. Shalf. The Cactus framework and toolkit: Design and applications. In *Vector and Parallel Processing – VECPAR'2002, 5th International Conference, Lecture Notes in Computer Science*, 2003.

[40] P. Goovaerts. *Geostatistics for Natural Resources Evaluation*. Applied Geostatics Series. 1997.

[41] B. Haasdonk, M. Dihlmann, and M. Ohlberger. A training set and multiple bases generation approach for parameterized model reduction based on adaptive grids in parameter space. *Mathematical and Computer Modelling of Dynamical Systems*, 17 (4):423–442, 2011.

[42] P. Holmes, J.L. Lumley, G. Berkooz, and C.W. Rowley. *Turbulence, Coherent Structures, Dynamical Systems and Symmetry*. Cambridge Monographs on Mechanics. Cambridge University Press, 2012.

[43] S. Hosder, R. W Walters, and R. Perez. A non-intrusive polynomial chaos method for uncertainty propagation in cfd simulations. volume 14, 2006.

[44] IFC2x3 TC1 Release. IFC Specification. *http://www.buildingsmart-tech.org/specifications/ifc-releases/ifc2x3-tc1-release/summary*.

[45] A. Inselberg. The plane with parallel coordinates. *The Visual Computer*, 1:69–91, 1985.

[46] E. H. Isaaks and R. M. Srivastava. *Applied Geostatistics*. Oxford University Press, 1989.

[47] John D Jakeman and Stephen G Roberts. Local and dimension adaptive sparse grid interpolation and quadrature. *arXiv preprint arXiv:1110.0010*, 2011.

[48] R. Jin, W. Chen, and T.W. Simpson. Comparative studies of metamodelling techniques under multiple modelling criteria. *Structural and Multidisciplinary Optimization*, 2001.

[49] C. Johnson, S. Parker, D. Weinstein, and S. Heffernan. Component-based, problem-solving environments for large-scale scientific computing. *Concurrency and Computation: Practice and Experience*, 14(13-15):1337–1349, 2002.

[50] D. R. Jones. A taxonomy of global optimization methods based on response surfaces. *Journal of global optimization*, 21(4):345–383, 2001.

[51] Donald R. Jones, Matthias Schonlau, and William J. Welch. Efficient global optimization of expensive black-box functions. *Journal of Global Optimization*, 13(4):455–492, December 1998.

[52] KAUST. Shaheen. *http://www.hpc.kaust.edu.sa*.

[53] D. Keim, J. Kohlhammer, G. Ellis, and F Mansmann. *Solving Problems with Visual Analytics*. 2012 (preprint).

[54] J. Knezevic, J. Frisch, R.-P. Mundani, and Rank. Interactive computing framework for engineering applications. *Journal of Computational Science*, 7(5):591–599, 2011.

[55] J. Knezevic, R.-P. Mundani, and E. Rank. Interactive computing – virtual planning of hip joint surgeries with real-time structure simulations. *International Journal of Modeling and Optimization*, 1(4):308–313, 2011.

[56] E. Lindholm, J. Nickolls, S. Oberman, and J. Montrym. Nvidia tesla: A unified graphics and computing architecture. *Micro, IEEE*, 28(2):39–55, 2008.

[57] G. J. A. Loeven, J. A. S. Witteveen, and H. Bijl. Probabilistic collocation: an efficient non-intrusive approach for arbitrarily distributed parametric uncertainties. volume 6, 2007.

[58] R. Marshall, J. Kempf, S. Dyer, and C.-C. Yen. Visualization methods and simulation steering for a 3d turbulence model of lake erie. In *Proceedings of the 1990 symposium on Interactive 3D graphics*, I3D '90, pages 89–97, 1990.

[59] K. Matkovic, D. Gracanin, M. Jelovic, and H. Hauser. Interactive visual steering - rapid visual prototyping of a common rail injection system. *IEEE Trans. Vis. Comput. Graph.*, 14(6):1699–1706, 2008.

[60] K. Matkovic, D. Gracanin, M. Jelovic, and Y. Cao. Adaptive interactive multi-resolution computational steering for complex engineering systems. In *EuroVA*, 2011.

[61] J. D. McCalpin. Stream: Sustainable memory bandwidth in high performance computers. Technical report, University of Virginia, 1991-2007.

[62] J. D. McCalpin. Memory bandwidth and machine balance in current high performance computers. *IEEE Computer Society Technical Committee on Computer Architecture (TCCA) Newsletter*, pages 19–25, 1995.

[63] B. H. McCormick, T. A. DeFanti, M. D. Brown, and R. Zaritsky. *Visualization in Scientific Computing*. SIGGRAPH video review. ACM SIGGRAPH, 1987.

[64] R. B. Miller. Response time in man-computer conversational transactions. In *Proceedings of the December 9-11, 1968, fall joint computer conference, part I*, pages 267–277, 1968.

[65] S. Molnar, M. Cox, D. Ellsworth, and H. Fuchs. A sorting classification of parallel rendering. *Computer Graphics and Applications, IEEE*, 14(4):23–32, 1994.

[66] B. Moore. Principal component analysis in linear systems: Controllability, observability, and model reduction. *Automatic Control, IEEE Transactions on*, 26(1):17–32, 1981.

[67] J. D. Mulder, J. J. Van Wijk, and R. Van Liere. A survey of computational steering environments. *Future Generation Computer Systems*, 13, 1998.

[68] A. Murarasu, J. Weidendorfer, G. Buse, D. Butnaru, and D. Pflüeger. Compact data structure and parallel algorithms for the sparse grid technique. In *16th ACM SIGPLAN Symposium on Principles and Practice of Parallel Programming*, 2011.

[69] R.H. Myers, D. C. Montgomery, and C.M. Anderson-Cook. *Response Surface Methodology: Process and Product Optimization Using Designed Experiments*. Wiley Series in Probability and Statistics. Wiley, 2009.

[70] J. Nickolls, I. Buck, M. Garland, and K. Skadron. Scalable parallel programming with cuda. *Queue*, 6(2):40–53, March 2008.

[71] B. Nouanesengsy, T.-Y. Lee, and H.-W. Shen. Load-balanced parallel streamline generation on large scale vector fields. *IEEE Transactions on Visualization and Computer Graphics*, 17(12):1785–1794, 2011.

[72] NVIDIA. *NVIDIA CUDA Programming Guide 2.0*. 2008.

[73] The OpenFOAM Foundation. OpenFOAM 2.1.1. http://www.openfoam.org.

[74] S. G. Parker. *The SCIRun problem solving environment and computational steering software system*. PhD thesis, The University of Utah, 1999.

[75] D. Pflüger. *Spatially Adaptive Sparse Grids for High-Dimensional Problems*. Verlag Dr. Hut, München, 2010.

[76] S. M. Pickles, R. Haines, R. L. Pinning, and A. R. Porter. A practical toolkit for computational steering. *Philosophical Trans. Royal Soc. London*, 363, 2005.

[77] R. Pinnau. Model reduction via proper orthogonal decomposition. In *Model Order Reduction: Theory, Research Aspects and Applications*, volume 13 of *Mathematics in Industry*, pages 95–109. Springer Berlin Heidelberg, 2008.

[78] Carden R. and Sorensen D. Automatic discrete empirical interpolation for nonlinear model reduction. Technical report, 2012.

[79] N. Richart, A. Esnard, and O. Coulaud. Toward a computational steering environment for legacy coupled simulations. In *Parallel and Distributed Computing, 2007. ISPDC '07. Sixth International Symposium on*, pages 43–43, 2007.

[80] G. Robertson, M. Czerwinski, P. Baudisch, B. Meyers, D. Robbins, G. Smith, and D. Tan. The large-display user experience. *IEEE Comput. Graph. Appl.*, 25(4):44–51, July 2005.

[81] A. Rosenfeld and A. C. Kak. *Digital picture processing*. Number v. 1 in Computer science and applied mathematics. Academic Press, 1982.

[82] G. Rozza and A.T. Patera. The heterogeneous thermal block problems. Technical report, 2008.

[83] J. Sacks, W. J. Welch, T. J. Mitchell, and H. P. Wynn. Design and analysis of computer experiments. *Statistical science*, 4(4): 409–423, 1989.

[84] A. Saltelli, S. Tarantola, F. Campolongo, and M. Ratto. *Sensitivity Analysis in Practice: A Guide to Assessing Scientific Models*. Wiley, 2004.

[85] B. Shneiderman. Response time and display rate in human performance with computers. *ACM Comput. Surv.*, 16(3):265–285, September 1984.

[86] M. A. Singer and W. H. Green. Using adaptive proper orthogonal decomposition to solve the reaction–diffusion equation. *Appl. Numer. Math.*, 59(2):272–279, February 2009.

[87] L. Sirovich. *Turbulence and the Dynamics of Coherent Structures.* Quarterly of applied mathematics. Brown University, Division of Applied Mathematics, 1987.

[88] M. Snir, S. Otto, S. Huss-Lederman, D. Walker, and J. Dongarra. *MPI-The Complete Reference, Volume 1: The MPI Core.* MIT Press, Cambridge, MA, USA, 2nd. (revised) edition, 1998.

[89] B. Sudret. Global sensitivity analysis using polynomial chaos expansions. *Reliability Engineering & System Safety*, 93(7):964–979, 2008.

[90] B. Sudret, M. Berveiller, and M. Lemaire. A stochastic finite element procedure for moment and reliability analysis. *European Journal of Computational Mechanics/Revue Européenne de Mécanique Numérique*, 15(7-8):825–866, 2006.

[91] J. K. Telford. A brief introduction to design of experiments. *Johns Hopkins Technical Digest*, 27(3):224–232, 2007.

[92] R. Van Liere and J. J. Van Wijk. Cse - a modular architecture for computational steering. In *Proceedings of the 7th Eurographics Workshop on Visualization in Scientific Computing*, pages 257–266. Springer Verlag, 1996.

[93] V. Varduhn, R.-P. Mundani, and E. Rank. Real time processing of large data sets from built infrastructure. *Journal of Systemics, Cybernetics and Informatics*, 9:63–67, 2011.

[94] V. Varduhn, R.-P. Mundani, and E. Rank. A framework for parallel numerical simulations on multi-scale geometries. In *Parallel and Distributed Computing (ISPDC), 2012 11th International Symposium on*, pages 274–278, 2012.

[95] J. S. Vetter and K. Schwan. High performance computational steering of physical simulations. In *Proceedings of the 11th International Symposium on Parallel Processing*, IPPS '97, pages 128–. IEEE Computer Society, 1997.

[96] K. Washabaugh, D. Amsallem, M. Zahr, and C. Farhat. Nonlinear model reduction for CFD problems using local reduced-order bases. In *42nd AIAA Fluid Dynamics Conference and Exhibit*, Fluid Dynamics and Co-located Conferences. American Institute of Aeronautics and Astronautics, June 2012.

[97] D. Xiu and G. Karniadakis. The wiener–askey polynomial chaos for stochastic differential equations. *SIAM J. Sci. Comput.*, 24(2):619–644, February 2002.

[98] D. Xiu and G. Karniadakis. Modeling uncertainty in flow simulations via generalized polynomial chaos. *Journal of Computational Physics*, 187(1):137–167, 2003.

[99] C. Zenger. Sparse grids. In Wolfgang Hackbusch, editor, *Parallel Algorithms for Partial Differential Equations*, volume 31 of *Notes on Numerical Fluid Mechanics*, pages 241–251. Vieweg, 1991.

[100] J. Zhang, J. Sun, Z. Jin, Y. Zhang, and Q. Zhai. Survey of parallel and distributed volume rendering: Revisited. In *Computational Science and Its Applications – ICCSA 2005*, volume 3482 of *Lecture Notes in Computer Science*, pages 435–444. Springer Berlin Heidelberg, 2005.

i want morebooks!

Buy your books fast and straightforward online - at one of world's fastest growing online book stores! Environmentally sound due to Print-on-Demand technologies.

Buy your books online at
www.get-morebooks.com

Kaufen Sie Ihre Bücher schnell und unkompliziert online – auf einer der am schnellsten wachsenden Buchhandelsplattformen weltweit! Dank Print-On-Demand umwelt- und ressourcenschonend produziert.

Bücher schneller online kaufen
www.morebooks.de

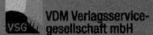

VDM Verlagsservicegesellschaft mbH
Heinrich-Böcking-Str. 6-8   Telefon: +49 681 3720 174   info@vdm-vsg.de
D - 66121 Saarbrücken   Telefax: +49 681 3720 1749   www.vdm-vsg.de

Printed by Books on Demand GmbH, Norderstedt / Germany